DESIGNING GARDENS ON SLOPES

Elizabeth Davies
&
Ruth Chivers

PACKARD PUBLISHING LIMITED

CHICHESTER

DESIGNING GARDENS ON SLOPES

Chapters 1 — 7 & 9 © Ruth E. Chivers
Chapter 8 © Elizabeth B. Davies

First published in 2012 by Packard Publishing Limited,
Forum House, Stirling Road, Chichester,
West Sussex, PO19 7DN, UK.

Second impression with revisions, December 2012

ISBN 978 1 84 531 138 0

Cover photo by Liz Davies.

Edited and prepared for press
by Michael Packard.

Designed by Newline Graphics,
Petworth, West Sussex.

Cover by Hilite Design & Reprographics,
Southampton, Hampshire, based on a
'house' style prepared by Louise Burston.

Printed and bound in the United Kingdom by
Publish Point, KnowledgePoint Limited,
Lower Earley, Reading, Berkshire.

Acknowledgements

Many thanks go to our clients and garden owners who have given permission to reproduce the designs for their gardens.

Julia Boulton for all her continuing support.

All plans, line drawings and photographs are by the Authors, with the exception of the following images whose photographers and designers are gratefully thanked:

This page:	Jerry Harpur, Harpur Garden Images;
	designer, Ulf Nordfjell.

Page iv	Designer, Keith Wiley.

Page 12:	Fiona McLeod, GAP Photos;
	designer, Paul Shaw.

Page 33:	Clive Nichols, GAP Photos;
	designer, Victor Shanley.

Page 34:	Fiona Lee, GAP Photos; courtesy St Andrews
	Botanic Garden, Scotland.

Page 35:	Jerry Harpur; courtesy RHS Garden,
	Hyde Hall, Essex.

Pages 42
& 80:	Rupert Davies for CAD graphics.

Page 46:	Jonathan Need, GAP Photos; courtesy Belasy
	Gardens, Northumberland.

Page 86:	Rob Whitworth, GAP Photos; designers, Haruko
	Seki, Makoto Saito & Locus Architects.

Page 87:	Fiona Lee, GAP Photos; courtesy
	St Andrews Botanic Garden, Scotland.

CONTENTS

Note: Each garden in Portfolio Chapter 8 has a selection of Sketches and Projections, and Presentation, Survey and Construction Plans

INTRODUCTION

The idea and inspiration for *Designing Gardens on Slopes* came from Liz. Living and working in Wales, designing gardens for over 18 years, she found that many of her clients had sloping gardens. With both of us having experience of problem solving on sloping sites, we decided to combine our knowledge and create this book. We wanted *Designing Gardens on Slopes* to give an overview of the practicalities of the whole process of designing a garden on a slope, from agreeing a client brief, through survey, sketch ideas, final design to seeing a completed garden, built and planted. We believe that seeing each step is really important in order to gain an understanding of how to solve the 'problem' of a sloping garden.

Many clients are daunted by the thought of how to tackle a change in level. Even relatively small slopes confound them, and steeper ground that seems to stretch endlessly away from the house in many different directions is more problematical. For Liz, hills have sometimes turned into mountain-sides, and she has even dealt with quarries. Often these sites have the most wonderful views, with real potential to make great gardens. But on a first visit, it is common to find there is nowhere actually to sit and enjoy the view — or if there is, it is in totally the wrong place. Luckier clients may have a well-placed window, and sometimes there may be a small 'shelf' of level space outside a door to sit on.

Our goal for this book is to show that rolling pieces of ground of all descriptions can be transformed with good design into wonderful spaces for outdoor living. Even in an unpredictable climate, sloping garden-owners today want gardens that really work for them: that is, functional outdoor spaces that look good all year round, from inside and outside.

The design of these curving retaining walls and steps belies the tight space into which they fit — just 5.5m by 18.3m — and makes transcending the fall of about 3m a delight.

Designing Gardens on Slopes starts with how to work up a feasible clients' brief, whatever they may want from their gardens. Each subsequent chapter provides a guide to thought processes and design techniques necessary in order to balance topographical, physical conditions with aesthetic design principles. In addition, it addresses issues such as balancing client expectations and budget constraints. Communication and education are two key parts of the role of garden and landscape designers. Liz designed all the gardens in the Chapter 8, Portfolio of Gardens. Most of them are small, fairly urban spaces: this is what the majority of owners of sloping gardens are faced with in our experience. These are real gardens for real people, not show gardens. Each project provides a detailed case study that demonstrates from start to finish exactly how to deal with the most important aspects of designing sloping gardens to achieve the best possible results. Other drawings to illustrate the text have been produced by Ruth. Finally, it is our experience that completing a sloping garden — designed, built and planted — involves a successful relationship between three people: the client, the designer, and the contractor.

E.B.D & R.E.C

1 THE DESIGN BRIEF

First Meeting with Clients

A sloping garden is often the very reason a garden designer is called in to resolve the additional challenges that changes in level present to garden owners. Even before the initial meeting with a client, a designer may get an impression of other similar sloping gardens in their client's neighbourhood, when the architectural style of local houses may be similar. A client's preferences may be influenced by these surroundings, and recognizing active dislikes can be equally helpful in establishing a successful working relationship between client and designer.

Some clients have an image in their minds of how they want their ideal garden to look. Others do not have a clue what they want, but know exactly what they don't either want or like in a garden. Teasing this information out of clients is part of a designer's job and the process starts initially by showing a portfolio of completed projects.

Portfolio and Budget

A designer's portfolio is an invaluable aid to kick-start the design process, and not least to get realistic budget figures under discussion with a potential client. With sloping gardens, it is essential that size of budget is established right from the start. Showing clients projects that are similar in all major aspects to their own garden helps them to understand both the scope of work involved and the amount of money required to construct features in the sloping garden. Many of these are necessary rather than elective, to underpin the whole garden, for example creating level areas with retaining walls and linking spaces with steps.

Landscape budgets are generally smaller than those for house renovation. This poses a greater problem for designers presented with sloping sites because of the costs related to all the important elements of construction: restricted access for machinery, earth moving, terracing with retaining walls and steps. Matching client expectations with their budgets is always important in any garden design project. Clients expect their designer to deliver results that not only meet their brief but also match their vision of an ideal garden. In sloping gardens balancing functionality, ease of use **and** aesthetics with budget constraints is a particular challenge.

Client Wish List to Design Brief

One way to ensure that a full brief is agreed with clients is to have a questionnaire or checklist that helps to identify their most important garden requirements and to establish priorities.

In sloping gardens, the age of users, mobility restrictions, access problems and drainage are all of increased significance. So by walking the site with the client, further information will be added such as their likes, dislikes, what they prefer to keep and what they see as disposable. These might not tally with a designer's preferences or initial ideas, but noting them at this stage ensures that all client preferences become part of the design brief. It may be, though, that some of them do not match up with good design principles, sound construction methods or size of budget. Garden surveys, however, will reveal more about the site and the underlying issues to be faced. While the design process develops, elements that designer and client differ upon will be negotiated and either deleted from the brief or retained but changed in a significant way. Client priorities may also change during the design process, so designers have to remain flexible, frustrating as that may be!

Examples of Site Information and a Client Brief

Site Information:

Size:	25m wide x 35m long = 875m²
Slope:	Ground runs down from the right to the left bottom corner.
Gradient:	3m from top to bottom, some cross fall.
Soil conditions:	None — no soil, disused agricultural buildings.
Budget:	Large.
Key features to be retained:	None.

Client Brief

- Parking required on top terrace nearest gates to road.
- Working area outside workshop.
- Access to small gate at bottom of site.
- Terraced garden that will provide areas of interest and privacy.
- A number of sitting areas.
- Lawn.
- Possible swim-pond to centre of site to harvest rainwater from buildings.
- Pool for fish.
- Summer kitchen/BBQ area to catch last of the evening sun in bottom left corner.
- Use reclaimed stone roof tiles from the barn in design of walls or steps.
- Lighting.
- Year-round interest in planting.
- Easy maintenance.

Budget and design brief

There can be a natural reticence to talk about money, that is, both design fees and building costs. So designers should discuss these issues from the start. Sloping gardens invariably require more construction costs, but continuing maintenance costs may also be higher, given the nature of the site. Discuss this early on as well because it affects design choices and fees as well as construction costs. Starting a process of cost-benefit analysis early on demonstrates how budgets can be balanced without reducing a new design. For example, show clients that it is a better use of a limited budget to keep an expensive item such as an existing retaining wall, of the right height and in the right place, rather than demolish and start again in a similar position using different materials. Existing walls can be re-finished to suit a design with paint, render, or re-faced with a different material.

On a first visit, in addition to talking to clients, house interiors also give indications of the overall style and look that they prefer. Walking the garden without the client allows the designer the opportunity to take pictures that will help with developing design ideas and to discover more about the site's true potential and instant reactions to it. When a sense of place is experienced, some initial ideas may lead on to become the foundations of the final design. However, they may have to be discarded once the site has been surveyed, levels taken and the full extent of the slope is realized. Early ideas, too, may have to be dismissed or scaled down when the available budget is clearly defined.

Taking a full brief from a client

Practicalities and Functions

1. *List* all garden users including pets, number and age of children.
2. *Garden negatives* include all existing functional issues: access problems, restricted mobility now or future – proofing, safety issues, lack of shady seating, too much sun, boundaries non-existent or in poor repair, eyesores that require screening, lack of privacy, prevailing winds, frost pockets.
3. *Garden positives* include all the pluses to be retained: views of the wider landscape, views to 'borrowed' landscape, buildings or trees in neighbours' gardens, good or distinctive architecture just beyond the site, e.g., church towers.
4. *Legal* – is the garden subject to planning approval? Is it in a Conservation Area or Area of Outstanding Natural Beauty (AONB); is the house a listed building? Some Residents' Associations want to see and approve garden plans; are trees protected by Tree Preservation Orders (TPOs)? Check any planning constraints with new-build houses, or covenants relating to the gardens of older properties, for example, hedges and fences not allowed in front gardens.
5. *Function* – what will the garden be used for: outdoor eating and entertaining, sun bathing, children and pets play, wildlife, plant collecting, hobby-gardening or other?
6. *Features* required and areas of space: fruit and vegetable growing, patio, compost bins, clothes drying, bins, log store, barbecue, water, summer house, conservatory added to house, car parking, greenhouse, shed, lawn, seating areas, viewing points, pergolas and other structures, lighting, irrigation.
7. *Maintenance* is really important. Who will maintain the garden and how much time will be required? If maintaining it themselves, how much work do clients want to do? Relate work levels with different styles of garden and amounts of planting.

Design and Aesthetics

8. *Style* – are different moods required in different areas? What does the clients' ideal garden look like – traditional, contemporary, minimalist, oriental, Mediterranean courtyard, cottage garden or other? Suggest that they keep images of things they like; develop a 'mood' board, with a palette of materials, plants and colours
9. *Planting* to suit the overall style; plant likes and dislikes – colours, shapes, types, aroma and fragrance (e.g., box and Ribes (flowering currant) exude distinctive smells that are commonly disliked).

Budget

10. *Budget* – not only the initial outlay on construction, but discuss ongoing maintenance, e.g., maintaining mature trees and hedges may incur sizable annual costs; how design factors affect design fees – some designers charge a percentage of total contract, others price for each project as a stand alone.

2 SURVEYING SLOPES

Surveying Sloping Gardens

Slopes greater than five per cent are visible to the eye *(see Table 2a)*. Distances between the house, existing garden features, trees and shrubs that are to be retained are measured in a linear site survey. In order to complete this as a base plan for a design for a sloping garden, all significant changes in ground level must be measured, recorded and added to complete a level survey.

At an initial site visit, note any visually obvious changes in level on a sketch plan of the garden. These are indicated by the tops of walls, fences and the number of any existing steps and are easily measured. Check that wall tops are flat. Note if fence panels slope with the ground or if they are stepped down with level tops. With steps, check whether the path top or bottom of them has been finished as a ramp. All of the above give an idea of the extent of the gradient change over a sloping garden, and are enough for the designer to proceed with giving a design fee quotation.

Successful designs for sloping gardens require complete accuracy. Carrying out your own garden survey can be achieved in a number of different ways and every designer has their own preferred method.

Some make a sketch plan on site then take measurements, record level changes and then draft the plans back in the office. Others draw up the complete survey on site. And some designers always get a professional survey done on any sloping site.

TABLE 2a EXPRESSING SLOPES IN DIFFERENT WAYS

Slope	Percentage %	Degrees °	Height of rise in Ground Level per 1m length in mm	
1:1	100	45	1000	STEEP
1:2	50	26.56	500	SLOPES
1:3	33.3	18.43	333	
1:4	25	14	250	
1:5	20	11.3	200	
1:6	16.6	9.46	166	
1:7	14.3	8.13	143	
1:8	12.5	7.12	125	SLOPING
1:9	11.1	6.34	111	GROUND
1:10	10	5.71	100	
1:11	9	5.19	90	
1:12	8.3	4.76	83	
1:13	7.7	4.39	77	
1:14	7.1	4.08	71	
1:15	6.6	3.91	67	
1:16	6.25	3.57	62.5	
1:20	5	2.86	50	'LEVEL'
1:25	4	2.29	40	GROUND
1:30	3.3	1.9	33	
1:40	2.5	1.43	25	
1:50	2	1.14	20	
1:60	1.6	0.95	16.6	

Measuring Levels

Slopes are surveyed and measured using three basic types of equipment. Professional surveyors mostly use a laser level where ground heights are measured by reading off the point at which the laser beam hits the measuring staff. Builders' levels are widely used and ground height is measured by placing a staff at key points and taking readings through the equipment's eye piece. A zip level provides a newer method of measuring slopes. Based on an altimeter similar to an aircraft's, it is operated by a single person. Once the instrument has been calibrated, no line of sight is required and no calculations are involved. Actual levels or elevation readings are shown on a digital display.

For the purposes of this book, the following section outlines level-surveying basics using a builder's level which is readily available for hire. The underlying principles relate to all sloping situations.

Whatever the method of garden survey, the basics of level measurement and recording on plans have to be understood by the designer. In large gardens and those with very complex levels, getting a professional survey carried out is the more efficient option. But the designer should add the position and measurements of all ground-floor doors and windows, which are not usually included on a professional survey unless surveyors are fully briefed on these requirements. The designer has also to name all the significant trees and plant groups that are to be retained on the survey plan, however it is drawn up.

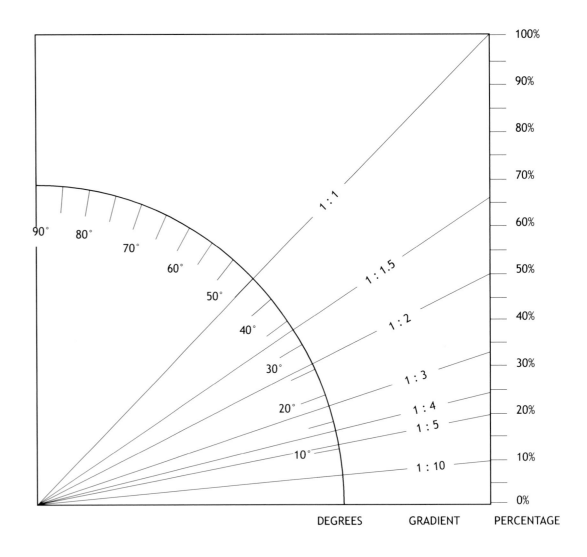

Figure 2.1 *Comparing the way slopes are expressed.*

Figure 2.2

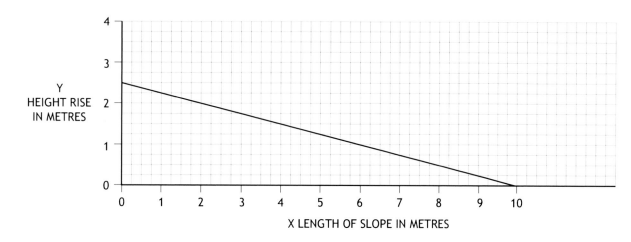

Y HEIGHT RISE IN METRES

X LENGTH OF SLOPE IN METRES

To work out a slope gradient expressed as 1:G

$G = \dfrac{X}{Y}$ or $G = \dfrac{\text{Length of Slope (X)}}{\text{Height Rise (Y)}}$

Example (see Fig. 2.2 above):

Garden slopes 2.5m over distance or length of 10m

Gradient (G) = $\dfrac{10\ (X)}{2.5\ (Y)}$ = 4 expressed as 1:4

Note 1: In Figs 2.2 & 2.3 both dimensions X and Y must be expressed in the same unit of measurement. Convert them first if they are not.

Note 2: 1:12, or 8.3%, is generally agreed to be a maximum gradient for a ramp for wheel-chair use in a public space, but 1:20, or 5%, is the preferred gradient.

To convert 1:G to a percentage (P%)

$P\% = \dfrac{100}{4}$

so 1:4 gradient becomes $\dfrac{100}{4}$ = 25%

To work out a gradient slope expressed as a percentage (P)

$P\% = \dfrac{Y \times 100}{X}$

Example (see Fig. 2.3 below):

Garden slopes 0.5m over distance or length of 6m.

$P\% = \dfrac{0.5\ (Y) \times 100}{6\ (X)}$ = 8.3%

To convert a percentage (P%) to a 1:G expression:

$G = \dfrac{100}{P\%}$, so 8.3% becomes $\dfrac{100}{8.3}$ = 12, or 1:12

Figure 2.3

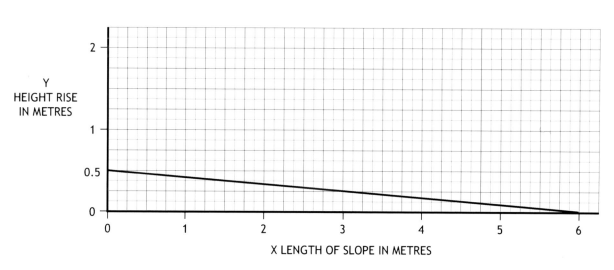

Y HEIGHT RISE IN METRES

X LENGTH OF SLOPE IN METRES

Level Surveying Basics

A full garden survey is completed using a level set up on a tripod — as used on construction sites. Having positioned equipment at a base station, ground levels are measured by placing the levelling staff at each key position in turn, viewing through the eyepiece and reading the height of the staff at the centre of the viewing lens. On a manual level, cross hairs align in the eyepiece at this position. With a laser level, the machine will read this off automatically. With either method, at each position the staff reading is noted down and spot level marked on the site sketch. Reduced levels are calculated before figures are noted on the final survey drawing (Fig. 2.5 & Table 2b).

Taking levels as well as measurements of linear distances at all survey points in a garden is not strictly necessary, but it does ensure that nothing is left out. The ground level at certain key positions influences proposed changes to the slope. Key positions for taking levels are at house corners and any other buildings, at doorways that open into the garden, on all drain covers, at the base of all trees and larger shrubs that are to be retained, at the top, mid-point and bottom of all visible slopes, at the base of any existing retaining walls, at the bottom and top of any existing steps, on any existing paved areas such as paths, patios and old shed bases.

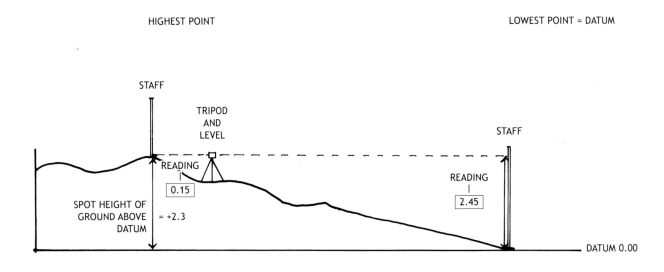

Figure 2.4

Surveying a sloping site with a builder's level on a tripod.

Readings are made at all key points, and these staff heights are noted.

To find the current height of the ground at each point, the reading at the low point becomes datum, and this figure is subtracted from each reading to give the reduced level, which is the height of the ground at that point relative to datum. Reduced levels are then shown on the survey plan.

For example, Reading 1 (2.45) minus Reading 2 (0.15) equals 2.3.

Therefore the ground level at that point is +2.3 metres above datum/lowest point.

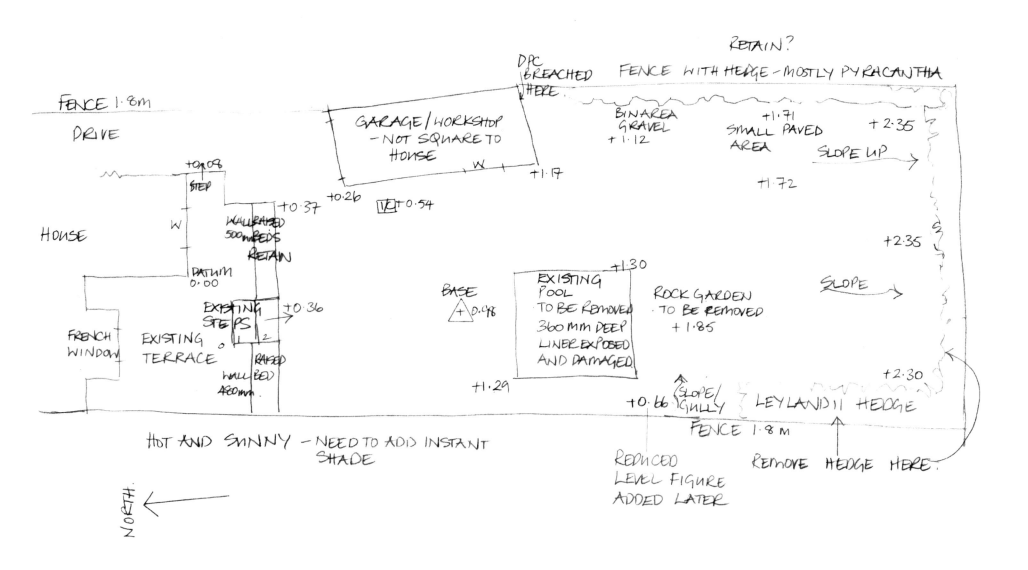

Figure 2.5

Designer's on-site sketch for survey showing all levels taken; this garden slopes up from the house by 2.35 metres.

Datum points and Reduced Levels

All changes in levels in a garden are measured in relation to a datum point. A datum point is also referred to as a temporary benchmark (TBM). On larger sites, the Ordnance Survey Bench Mark (OSBM), as seen marked BM on OS maps, refers to the ground height above sea level. Professional garden site surveys will indicate whether a datum is arbitrary and which benchmarks are used.

When designers carry out their own survey, the datum can be any point that will not be changed by proposed groundworks, for example a drain cover, the floor level at a doorway into the garden, the house or other building's DPC, or an existing step. As measurements of level change are relative to this datum point, each position is subtracted from the datum height to produce reduced levels. It is these reduced level figures that are noted on the survey plan. Using this method results in positive and negative figures, and these can give rise to confusion when reading plans. Alternatively, by making the datum point the lowest position on the site, all reduced level figures will be positive. This makes ground-level height changes very clear, as it is these figures that will be used when calculating where to cut and fill the slope, where retaining walls are to be built, their heights, and the number and height of steps.

Professional surveys show existing ground contours and their gradients in addition to spot levels across the (Figs 2.6) site.

TABLE 2b SURVEY: WORK SHEET

Property: **Example**

Base: **Eye Level 1:47**
Reduced Level: **0.98**

Point	Location	Height (Staff Reading)	Reduced Level +	
A	Top left corner	0.1	2.35	(Datum – Reading 2.45 – 0.1)
B	Mid top of garden	0.15	2.30	
C	Top right corner	0.15	2.30	
D	Middle of mid area	0.68	1.77	
E	Front R. of paved space	0.73	1.72	
F	Front L. of paved area	0.74	1.71	
G	Rockery	0.6	1.85	
H	Boundary (ground falls away)	1.79	0.66	
I	Pool – back corner	1.15	1.30	
J	Gravel bin area	1.33	1.12	
K	Back of garage	1.28	1.17	
L	Pool – front corner	1.16	1.29	
M	Inspection cover	1.91	0.54	
N	Front of garage	2.19	0.26	
O	Middle of route (from steps)	1.98	0.47	
P	Boundary/raised bed	1.99	0.46	
Q	Top step (middle)	2.09	0.36	
R	L/H raised bed corner	2.08	0.37	
S	House corner 1	2.37	0.08	
T	House corner 2	2.45	0.00	DATUM
U	House corner 3	2.42	0.03	
V	Mid-terrace (paving)	2.44	0.01	

Datum: Highest staff reading is the lowest point on site.

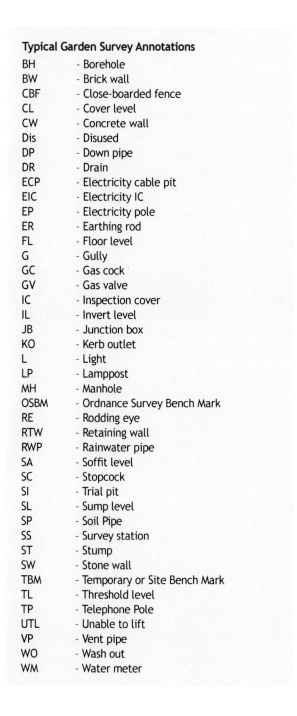

Typical Garden Survey Annotations

BH	- Borehole
BW	- Brick wall
CBF	- Close-boarded fence
CL	- Cover level
CW	- Concrete wall
Dis	- Disused
DP	- Down pipe
DR	- Drain
ECP	- Electricity cable pit
EIC	- Electricity IC
EP	- Electricity pole
ER	- Earthing rod
FL	- Floor level
G	- Gully
GC	- Gas cock
GV	- Gas valve
IC	- Inspection cover
IL	- Invert level
JB	- Junction box
KO	- Kerb outlet
L	- Light
LP	- Lamppost
MH	- Manhole
OSBM	- Ordnance Survey Bench Mark
RE	- Rodding eye
RTW	- Retaining wall
RWP	- Rainwater pipe
SA	- Soffit level
SC	- Stopcock
SI	- Trial pit
SL	- Sump level
SP	- Soil Pipe
SS	- Survey station
ST	- Stump
SW	- Stone wall
TBM	- Temporary or Site Bench Mark
TL	- Threshold level
TP	- Telephone Pole
UTL	- Unable to lift
VP	- Vent pipe
WO	- Wash out
WM	- Water meter

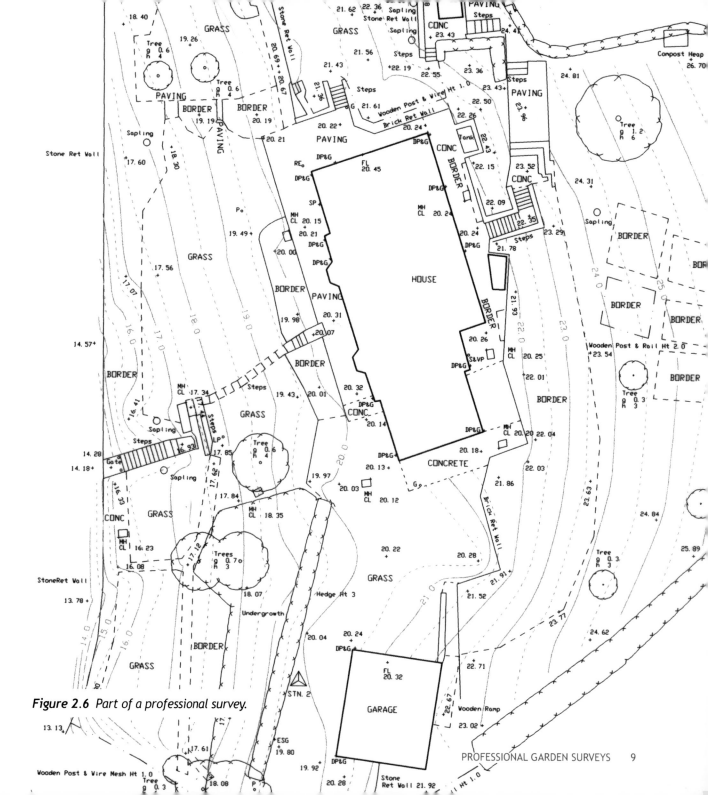

Figure 2.6 *Part of a professional survey.*

On steeper slopes and with larger gardens, include contours on the survey drawing or make a separate contour plan to overlay outline designs. This ensures a design follows the natural contours of the site rather than reshaping the whole slope.

Figure 2.7

Slope Contours – Existing

- *Professional surveys may show contours with a solid line and a height above the Datum point written through it.*

- *Spot levels are measured heights relative to Datum and shown on plan.*

- *Existing contours are shown as a broken line.*

- *Gradient – the closer the contour lines, the steeper the gradient.*

Slope Contours – Proposed

- *Proposed contours are shown with shorter dashes of broken lines.*

- *Current levels are shown marked CL, usually in brackets. Both are ground heights relative to a Datum height or level.*

- *Ground shaping is usually refined on site; therefore this is a key time when the designer should be present.*

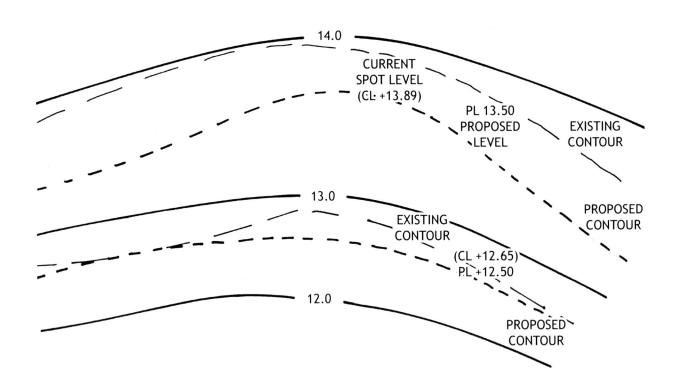

Recording Relevant Information

Not all changes in level on a site are relevant to a garden design. For example, a spot level is not strictly required if a bank or existing terrace is to remain unchanged in the new design. But if such areas are adjacent to proposed earthworks, this information will be needed.

It is better to over-record than skimp on details. To ensure that all key level changes are measured and recorded, a simple sketch of the site notes where each base station of the level and tripod was established, and where each spot level was taken.

A detailed discussion of surveying a garden is beyond the scope of this book. For more detailed information see *Surveying for Garden Designers* by Ian Humby or *Surveying for Construction* by William Irvine and Finlay Maclennon.

Surveying slopes – summary of essential Information

- *Degree of slope* – garden slopes can be divided into these broad categories: flat, sloping, steep and complex. Each has its own design implications since few gardens are completely flat. Slope is defined in several ways: degrees (°), gradient expressed as a ratio 1:rate of rise, and as a percentage (%) (see Fig. 2.3).
- *Level ground can appear level* to the naked eye, but it is rare to find a garden that is dead flat. Level ground may have a slope of 5% or less – approximately 2.86° – or a gradient up to 1:20.
- *Sloping ground* – undulating or rolling ground occurs in gardens with visible slopes of 10 to 12%. It is possible to move around on this degree of sloping ground, but there may not be a large enough expanse of level space to sit or to put a pool of water.
- *Steep slopes* are more than 12% or 12m in 100m, or 3.6m in 30m. Gardens with this scale of slope are the most expensive to develop. Soils can also be thin, accompanied by rocky ground.
- *Complex slopes* occur where the ground slopes in more than one direction across the site.
- *Damp Proof Course (DPC)* – note where this is on the house and on any other buildings in the garden. DPCs must never be breached by ground levels. All ground levels and paved areas should be finished 150mm below the level of a DPC.
- *Important existing levels* are all noted on the garden survey. Key positions include: at the corners of the house and any other buildings; at doorways that open into the garden; drain covers; at the base of all trees and larger shrubs that are to be retained; at the top, mid-point and bottom of all visible slopes; at the base of existing retaining walls; at the bottom and top of any existing steps; on any existing paved areas such as paths, patios, old shed bases, etc.
- *Sill heights of doors into the garden* – measure these because they may affect choice of hard-landscaping materials; e.g., decking may be chosen for a solid external surface just below a door sill.
- *Professional garden surveys* by specialists should be used in large gardens or for very complex slopes, but designers still need to make their own notes about the site, including areas with poor drainage, fine views out of the garden, eyesores that require screening, and prevailing winds. The position and dimensions of all doors and windows into the garden are also noted on the final survey as they will influence a good design.
- *Designer's completion* of survey or presence at it; going back to a site is always a great advantage. Measuring and making notes provides an opportunity to gain a deeper understanding of the garden and a feel for the space from every angle.
- *Legal constraints and considerations* – consult the local authority planning department at the start of the process if there is any doubt about listed building status, AONB or Conservation Areas.
- *Trees* – details about earth moving around existing trees are in Chapter 5.

A 'borrowed' landscape: the changing pattern of farmland and woods beyond the garden.

3 COMMUNICATING DESIGN IDEAS

Functional Basics

Making or enlarging level areas in sloping gardens is usually a priority. Sometimes the house itself needs anchoring into the site by creating a large level area around it. Patios, play areas, water, summer-houses, sheds, greenhouses and ornamental planting require level space. There are three methods of making level areas on a slope: cut and fill, the process of moving soil on site; using soil brought in to the site; a raised platform or timber deck is built over the slope. The first two methods usually require building retaining walls; the last requires support by a well-engineered system of strong posts and sound structural framework. For further information about cut and fill, see Chapter 5 Groundworks and Construction.

Designing for slopes

All the best gardens have a real sense of place. Most of them acknowledge the surrounding landscapes and any existing architectural features. Take in what lies beyond the garden boundaries. A lack of inspiring views may not have a great influence on the design, and so the garden can be planted in any style to suit the client's requirements and design brief, provided that location, weather and soil conditions are all taken into account with plant selection. If, when looking out from the garden, the views are of 'natural' landscape, allow the planting towards the garden boundary to meld with and reflect the landscape that stretches beyond it towards the horizon. Surrounding landscapes may be beautiful whether they are of the unspoiled beauty of nature or a man-made and managed version of it. Agricultural fields can have beautiful ground forms, contrasting textural patterns and colour schemes that change throughout the year. Don't fight fine views of any kind. Design with a light hand, and keep it simple

and minimal. In order to achieve this effect, position retaining walls, steps, paths and paved areas where they fit more naturally into the site. Choose materials for all hard surfaces that harmonize with the house and the surrounding landscape.

Today, many designers use CAD and other software for some or all parts of the design process. Good design principles are universal and hold true whether designs are hand-drafted, computer-generated or a combination of the two methods. So design the garden paying attention to how the house sits in the space. All ground-floor doors leading into the garden, and windows looking out on to it, should relate to the position of terraces, patios, paths and planting. Measuring the house accurately at the survey stage is the key to achieving this result, and it is only reached if the positions and dimensions of house doors and windows are put on the survey plan. Relating the centre lines of these is important, for both practical and aesthetic reasons. For good access, align paths with doorways. Make good views a priority from windows. Taller plants should not obscure views or create a barrier between the garden and the house where this is not part of the design brief. Place retaining walls with care: close to the house, they should be no higher than necessary to create areas of open space. Some designers use a grid system, based on the dimensions of doors, windows or other features of the house footprint, and this forms the basis of the spatial arrangement and proportions of their designs *(Figs. 3.1 to 5)*. The same technique is employed in sloping gardens to scale terraces and patios by positioning retaining walls, steps and paths to align with the underlying grid adopted.

Looking into a garden from a higher terrace.

Design Principles

Proportion, scale, harmony, rhythm, repetition, textural contrast and focal points apply to the design of all gardens, including sloping ones. Design the garden working out from the house. Make the adjoining level space in scale with the size of the building behind it. In general, follow the guidelines on dimensions described in the box to the right for elements such as patios, paths and steps. But these are only guidelines; actual scale and proportions of features are determined by the size of each garden. A sense of rhythm adds movement to a garden. Creating good circulation around the sloping site is important for clients. Combine this with adding a sense of rhythm by repeating elements such as a flight of steps, or planting a row of a single plant — trees, shrubs or a taller grass — or repeating the same plant in similar positions throughout the garden; for example, at the apex of a curve, at the top and bottom of steps, or at the junction of two paths. Highlight necessary features such as retaining walls and steps to make them interesting as well as functional. Choose materials, finishes and colours with equal care.

For inspiration, visit both public and private gardens on sloping sites, which range from the grand to the more homely. Looking at real gardens helps increase an understanding of how changes in level work. Notice the scale of each space, the materials used on the ground, retaining walls and steps, and how each level connects to the rest. Experience the height of step risers, depth of treads, and width of the flight — notice how stride pattern is affected. On steeper slopes, have enough landings been created? Is circulation round the garden a pleasing experience? Perhaps movement is not totally comfortable, or worse still, feels unsafe. Observe how steps may twist and turn to create intrigue and affect mood; how walls are placed, what they are built from and whether they are in harmony with their surroundings; how even small changes in level add interest to any site. Any one of many details can be an inspiration, to be adapted for use in your own designs. Most importantly, notice the things that do not look good and do not work in the overall design. The adoption of an almost forensic approach to garden visiting will help you to understand the design of gardens in general. It can be a very useful aid to avoiding costly errors with designs for sloping gardens.

Dimensions of Key Features

Patios

3 to 3.5m square giving total area of 9m² to 12.25m² allows space for a table and 6 chairs to be pulled out around it. Make patios as generous as site allows.

Secondary seating spaces can be smaller, more intimate, in scale with the surrounding area and their place in the overall design.

Paths

All paths do not carry the same 'weight' in a design. For paved main paths, 1m width is a minimum, 1.2m is better by allowing 2 people to walk side-by-side, 1.5m is more generous. Make paths wider where abundant planting will overhang them.

In general, make path widths suitable to their function: the more frequently travelled, the wider the garden path. Mysterious, quieter, more solitary paths can be narrower and not necessarily solid paved. Overall, design paths in scale with the site.

Steps

Garden steps should have the same width as the paths leading to them. Width of steps and landings also depends on frequency of use and the number of people using them. Riser height of 150mm to 180mm maximum is recommended. All risers in a flight should be the same height, with all treads the same depth. Minimum riser height is 100mm. Scale of steps should relate to garden size. Demarcation of tread and riser should be clear and treads should have good slip-resistant properties. For more information on step design, see Chapter 6.

Retaining Walls

For retaining walls above 1m in height, take advice from a structural engineer. An experienced landscape contractor can advise about lower walls. Where roads adjoin a sloping garden, take advice from a surveyor. Depending on proximity to public highway and slope gradient, excavation work may require planning permission. Always take professional advice with steep slopes — any excavation on site may require steel reinforcements. For more information on retaining walls, see Chapter 6.

Raised Terraces, Decks and Platforms

Garden surfaces higher than 600mm above surrounding levels are subject to regulations that require them to have a 900mm high barrier around them for safety purposes. Fences, walls, toughened glass, stainless steel balustrade or railings are all suitable options.

For more on safety issues, see Chapter 6.

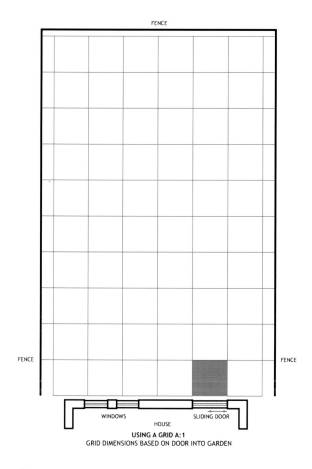

FENCE

WINDOWS   SLIDING DOOR

HOUSE

USING A GRID A:1
GRID DIMENSIONS BASED ON DOOR INTO GARDEN

FENCE   FENCE

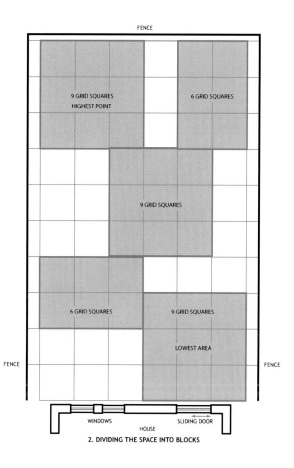

FENCE

9 GRID SQUARES
HIGHEST POINT

6 GRID SQUARES

9 GRID SQUARES

6 GRID SQUARES

9 GRID SQUARES

LOWEST AREA

FENCE   FENCE

WINDOWS   SLIDING DOOR

HOUSE

2. DIVIDING THE SPACE INTO BLOCKS

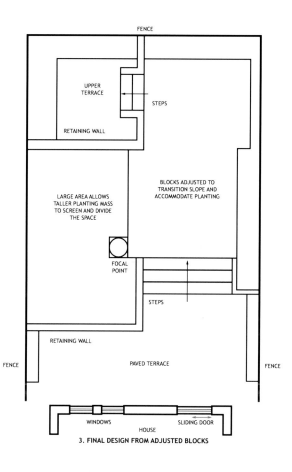

FENCE

UPPER
TERRACE

STEPS

RETAINING WALL

BLOCKS ADJUSTED TO
TRANSITION SLOPE AND
ACCOMMODATE PLANTING

LARGE AREA ALLOWS
TALLER PLANTING MASS
TO SCREEN AND DIVIDE
THE SPACE

FOCAL
POINT

STEPS

RETAINING WALL

FENCE   PAVED TERRACE   FENCE

WINDOWS   SLIDING DOOR

HOUSE

3. FINAL DESIGN FROM ADJUSTED BLOCKS

Figure 3.1 A grid is drawn with the vertical lines derived from the dimensions of the door into the garden, which is the dominant feature of the house elevation facing into the garden. Horizontal lines start on the back wall of the house. The grid works in relation to the house, not to the boundaries.

Figure 3.2 Multiples of grid squares make blocks that are used to delineate different areas of the garden. They also create ground patterns. Scale and harmony derive from the correct proportions of the blocks. In this example, three blocks of nine grid squares enable transition from the lowest area to the highest point. Smaller blocks ensure balance to the design. The grid can then be discarded.

Figure 3.3 The blocks that underpin the design are adjusted. In this way existing plants, or other features, can be retained but the final design will remain true to the proportions of the blocks and ultimately the house — on which the grid was based and the blocks derived.

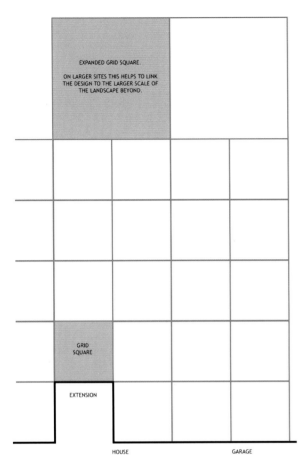

USING A GRID B
GRID SCALED FROM THE DIMENSIONS OF THE HOUSE EXTENSION ·
THE DOMINANT ARCHITECTURAL FEATURE.

Figure 3.4 On larger sites, a grid based on the architectural features of the house can be expanded as the garden reaches its boundaries. Doubling or quadrupling the original grid square unit means that the design's 'building blocks' derived from it will relate the final design to the larger scale of the landscape beyond the garden boundaries. Relating a garden to the surrounding landscape ensures that the site is in harmony.

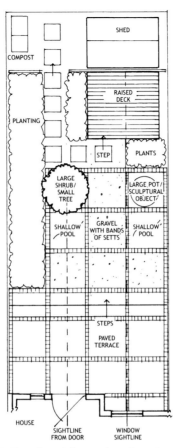

Figure 3.5 Showing sight or view lines from doors and windows into the garden when initial design ideas were evolved, ensures that key features align with the house. For example, steps up or down from a terrace enable easier garden access if they align with a door, and the same is true for garden paths, particularly main routes that are used every day.

Here, a taller plant is placed as a feature creating planting height and holding the eye within the main garden. Paving detail that aligns with the centre of the window accentuates the longest view into the space. Coincidentally, a grid based on the door-width forms the dominant ground pattern in this small garden.

One Garden — Three Ideas

This small terraced house is elevated above its gently sloping garden. Existing steps provided access to the lower level. The garden boundary is a low stone wall.

Design Brief

- A strong design — the main view of the garden is from the house above.
- Seating in the lower area of the garden.
- Retain shed in its current position.
- Retain interest within the garden.
- Take full advantage of the 70cm slope.

Design 1 — Formal

Single-axis garden on three levels with formal shapes — the circular area holds the eye within the garden. Brick edging matches the house and paving is kept to a minimum, to keep costs down. Four single steps define the areas. A pair of topiary trees forms the entrance to the end section. Slight changes in ground level are easily lost in borders once they are graded and planted.

Design 2 — Diagonal Garden

Setting the design at this angle can make narrow sites appear wider. This amount of hard landscaping results in less maintenance. Levelling the space and paving involves removing excess soil from the site, which increases costs. A water feature in the middle section is a strong focal point that retains interest inside the space.

Design 3 — Informal Curves

The slope flows gently down through a rustic arch to an enclosed, hidden seating area. Two trees add a sense of depth, additional height and screening. It is a calm space and the most economical of the three designs, because there are no steps to build, levelling is minimal, and reclaimed paving is already on site.

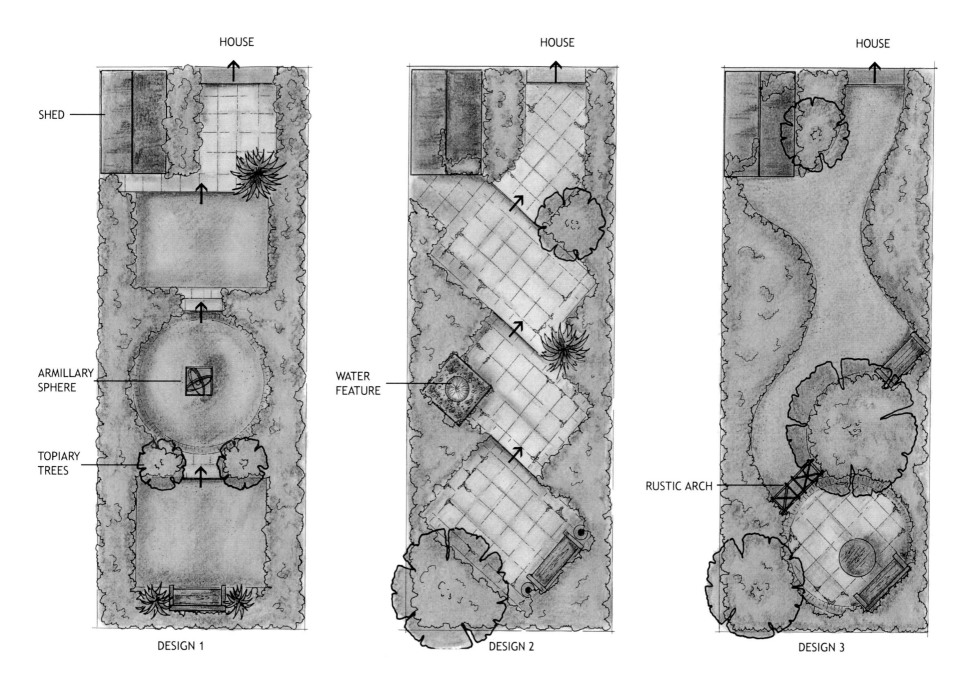

HOUSE

HOUSE

HOUSE

SHED

ARMILLARY
SPHERE

TOPIARY
TREES

WATER
FEATURE

RUSTIC ARCH

DESIGN 1

DESIGN 2

DESIGN 3

Summary — Design Idea Essentials

- *Budget* — plays a key part in implementing a design in sloping gardens. Ground works, levelling, drainage, retaining walls and steps all take up a significant amount of available budget, whatever materials are used.

- *Lie of the land* — shape of the ground and nature of the slope are important to the finished design. Go with the 'flow' of ground contours wherever feasible, to make as light as mark as possible on the landscape.

- *Avoid over-terracing* and building too many or very tall retaining walls; it's very costly and not good aesthetically. As a general rule, let the design follow the natural contours rather than reshape the whole slope.

- *Immovable existing features* — whether buildings, hard landscaping, trees or other planting — usually dictate how a new design will fit the site and the location of new features.

- *Views out of the garden* — retain fine views out and 'frame' them with suitable planting. Do not plant trees or plan large features to block a good view.

- *Views inside the garden* — use the centre lines of ground-floor doors and windows leading on to the garden to ensure that a new design creates good views and focal points. Use this technique to create an informal garden without axes. For the symmetry of classical formal design, balance the layout around a single central axis.

- *Drainage problems* can be common on sloping sites. Design features such as rainwater gardens, gullies and planted swales provide possible solutions. For more information on water management techniques, see *Rain Gardens*, by Nigel Dunnett and Andy Clayden.

- *Initial onsite sketches* are invaluable. Frequently, a first response to a sloping site will be the one that is worked up to a final design.

- *Make plenty of sketches* of different ideas or concepts — there is always more than one design solution. Experiment with curving, rectangular and angular approaches.

- *Encourage clients* to be engaged in the project. Ask them to collect images of features, materials and plants they like as well as pictures of gardens with the type of atmosphere they would like to see in their own garden.

- *Formulate ideas* and communicate them to clients; inspire them with how the changes will look. Getting clients to focus is also part of a designer's job.

4 DESIGN PRESENTATION

Communicating the Design

Many clients do not understand scale plans, yet they are essential to garden design. A plan has to communicate design ideas and solutions to the client. It should contain as much information as possible to 'sell' the new design in order to convince clients that all the problems of their sloping site have been addressed. It must convey the message that the designer has understood their brief and that the finished design takes into account all of their garden requirements and how they will use the space after completion. Contractors need plans as a basis for their quotations; then as a 'blueprint' for building the garden.

For many clients, rough thumbnail sketches of areas of the proposed design are more easily understood. Simple hand-drawn overlays over a photograph can help to explain a new garden design to clients, and to envisage how the space will look when completed (*Fig. 4.1*). The information box on p.22 highlights the most important ways in which garden design plans can be made easier to understand. These apply whether working with CAD or hand-drawn plans.

Section drawings are another way of communicating the way changes are made in sloping gardens. Using these drawings, a designer can help clients envisage the new garden design (*Fig. 4.2*).

Figure 4.1 Simple sketch overlays provide a quick and easy way to communicate design ideas. They enable clients to visualize planned changes.

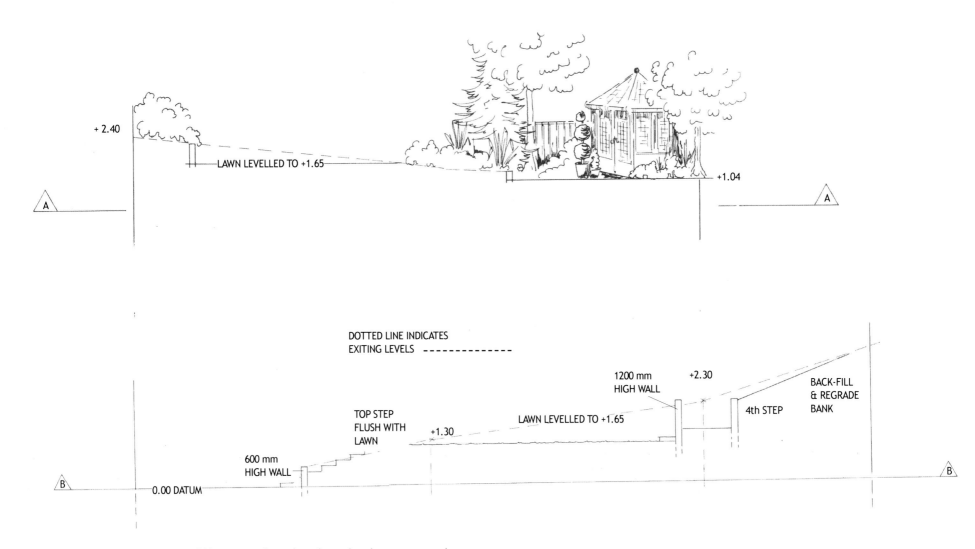

+ 2.40

LAWN LEVELLED TO +1.65

+1.04

A

A

DOTTED LINE INDICATES
EXITING LEVELS - - - - - - - - - - - - - - -

1200 mm
HIGH WALL

+2.30

BACK-FILL
& REGRADE
BANK

TOP STEP
FLUSH WITH
LAWN

+1.30

LAWN LEVELLED TO +1.65

4th STEP

600 mm
HIGH WALL

B

B

0.00 DATUM

Figure 4.2 Sections from two different gardens that show the changes to gardens
will also help clients to visualize a range of new layouts. See Chapter 8 for sequential
proposed sections and projections for actual sloping gardens.

Making plans easier to understand or 'read'

Variation of the thickness of lines helps to make a plan easier to understand, whether plans are CAD-generated or hand-drafted. Doing this also brings a one-dimensional drawing to life. Taller features and plants are shown with a thicker line, so giving a better impression of the varying heights and comparative bulk of the finished garden.

Ground shaping

Some sites and situations lend themselves to the use of ground forms to re-shape the slope, almost sculpting levelled areas out of it. Berms and embankments are the main methods of achieving this, and the designer's intentions can be shown in a separate ground works plan. This is a guide, used for communicating ideas and as a basis for costing. Realizing ground forms is best when fine-tuned on site when the excavations actually are underway (Figs. 4.4 & 4.5).

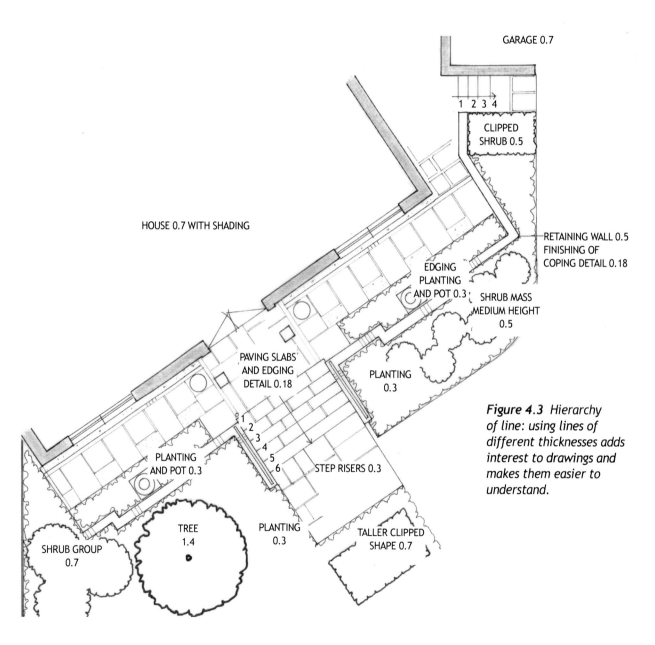

GARAGE 0.7

CLIPPED SHRUB 0.5

HOUSE 0.7 WITH SHADING

RETAINING WALL 0.5 FINISHING OF COPING DETAIL 0.18

EDGING PLANTING AND POT 0.3

SHRUB MASS MEDIUM HEIGHT 0.5

PAVING SLABS AND EDGING DETAIL 0.18

PLANTING 0.3

PLANTING AND POT 0.3

STEP RISERS 0.3

SHRUB GROUP 0.7

TREE 1.4

PLANTING 0.3

TALLER CLIPPED SHAPE 0.7

Figure 4.3 Hierarchy of line: using lines of different thicknesses adds interest to drawings and makes them easier to understand.

BERMS

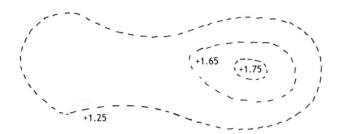

Figure 4.4 *Berms, or man-made mounds, can be used as a means of re-grading slopes, and as part of the methods of dealing with issues of drainage and groundwater.*

EMBANKMENTS

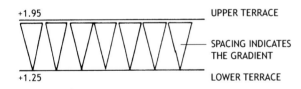

CURVING EMBANKMENTS ARE INFORMAL, MORE NATURALISTIC, AND THE GRADIENT CAN VARY.

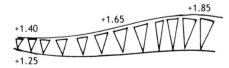

Figure 4.5 *Existing and proposed embankments are shown in the same way.*

Design Presentation

- *Scale plans* must be accurate so that finished gardens match the designs. Usually, more than one plan is required: a presentation plan, that may be coloured, is for the client; a working plan that shows dimensions and setting out points is for contractors to make detailed quotations for building the garden and implementing the design; overlays and projections are aids to visualisation for everyone *(Fig. 4.1)*; sections through sloping gardens show the impact of changes of level *(Fig. 4.2)*. See Chapter 8 for sequences of presentations and plans for actual gardens.

- *Plans* should be clear. Use accepted notation to clarify all changes. Note on plan what Datum has been used, and show the proposed ground levels with a plus or minus sign relative to that point.

- *Hierarchy of line* — a variation of line thickness makes a plan easier to understand and read. Use thicker lines for taller features. Using a heavier weight of line for retaining walls and step treads highlights changes in levels *(Fig. 4.3)*.

- *Retaining and freestanding walls* — draw with a thicker line. Show finished heights on the plan. For complete accuracy, construction drawings of scale 1:20 or 1:10 may be required in addition to the plan, and definitely for planning applications. Construction drawings give full details of foundations, materials, copings, finishes — everything required to build all features shown on the plan.

- *Steps* — draw to show the exact number and depth of treads. Arrows point up a flight of steps, never down. Number risers in sequence, and show any side retaining walls and handrails if these are part of the design. Labelling steps with an 'Up' sign underlines their function. Heights of each riser can be notated on the drawing or included as a note in an information box on the side of the plan. *See Chapter 6.*

- *Ramps* — show with an arrow pointing in the upward direction. Indicate spot ground levels top and bottom of the ramp. Include the gradient or angle of the ramp's rise.

- *Utilities* include manhole covers on a working drawing for contractors. These affect level changes whatever material surrounds them. Position of drains leading to septic tanks, other water treatment utilities and routes of power cables and gas supplies should be shown; all of these affect where walls are built, how the ground surface is treated and where trees, hedges and other larger plants are planted.

- *Ground forms and contouring* — with larger gardens and steep slopes a separate contour plan shows significant ground reshaping and helps fit the design to the slope. Areas of new mounds and berms *(Fig. 4.4)* are shown with the ground level labelled at the proposed highest and lowest points. Embankments *(Fig. 4.5)* are marked on plan in the conventional way; the length of arrows indicates the extent of the slope. A plan that shows this detailed information on ground levels is an invaluable guide to the planning of earth movement. But groundworks of whatever scale are invariably finalized with the designer on site during process of setting out and excavation.

5 GROUND WORKS AND CONSTRUCTION

All gardens need solid construction. Ground works on slopes lay the foundations for the whole garden, not just for each feature in isolation, because all changes have to work together. Construction, therefore, includes substantial excavation and any other alteration of the slope, from the simplest re-grading of soil through to cut and fill to make new level areas.

Cut and Fill

The three methods of making level areas on a slope are:

- to excavate and move the soil on site, rearranging it to create a level space or terrace; this is commonly known as cut and fill;
- soil is brought to the site and the existing gradient is re-graded to create level space;
- a timber deck is constructed to make a raised platform that cantilevers from a higher point over a lower area.

Cut and fill is the most commonly used method to create level spaces in sloping gardens. The principles are shown in *Figs. 5.1* and *5.2*.

GROUNDWORKS - CUT AND FILL 1

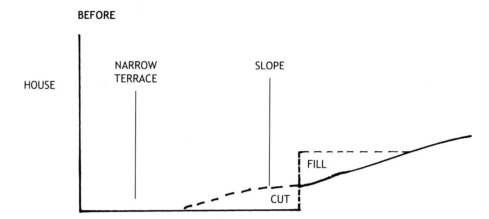

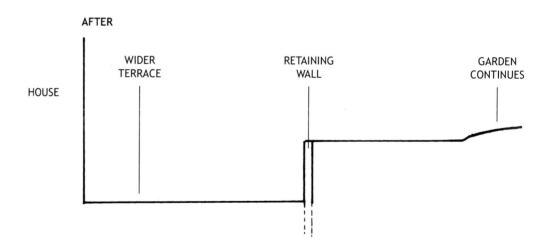

Figure 5.1 *Position retaining walls with care. Keep their height to a minimum. In many cases, two lower retaining walls will give better-finished results than one taller one, but avoid over-terracing the site.*

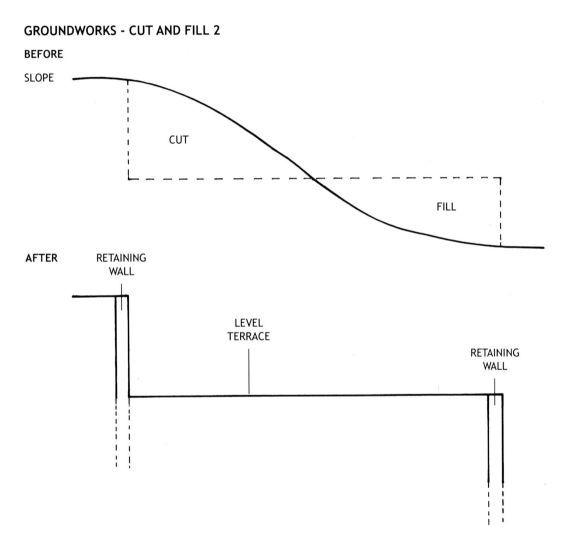

GROUNDWORKS - CUT AND FILL 2

BEFORE

SLOPE

CUT

FILL

AFTER

RETAINING WALL

LEVEL TERRACE

RETAINING WALL

Figure 5.2 Balance the volumes of cut and fill where possible to avoid removal of unwanted soil or importing new soil to the site. Both are costly.

Mistakes to Avoid

- Removal of too much soil from site and having to import it back is costly, and soil types may not match, soil quality might be unknown. Check calculations and take expert advice.

- Schemes that involve bringing large amounts of soil into the garden are expensive, and the provenance of imported soil is unknown.

- Failing to reinforce areas when terraces are being created with made up soil.

- Failure to store topsoil removed before excavation starts. The soil should be stored separately in as low a mound as possible to maintain optimum soil structure.

Moving soil and constructing around trees

During ground works and construction, care must be taken not to compromise the root systems of mature trees if they are to be retained on site. A certified tree surgeon or arboriculturist should carry out a tree survey, and report whether trees are protected by Tree Preservation Orders (TPOs), in a Conservation Area or Area of Outstanding Natural Beauty (AONB). The resulting report will detail the following information:

- Reference tag with location of tree on site map;

- Species;

- Size — including height, crown spread of tree at 4 cardinal points and clearance of canopy from ground;

- Maturity and life expectancy — estimate of remaining years, assuming continued maintenance;

- Condition of tree — using A to C ratings and R for Redundant or Remove rating, based on the amenity value attributed to each specimen;
- Notes on recommended management.

The arboriculturist will also review the impact that proposed site excavation will make on existing trees. Impact assessment will enable design plans to be finalized: the position of retained trees affects where the ground is excavated. A Tree Protection Plan should follow a tree assessment report, and relates the tree survey to the design proposal. This will clearly indicate trees to be retained in the new design and trees that are to be removed, either through their condition or felled to make design implementation possible. Each Root Protection Area (RPA) of a tree that is to be retained should be calculated, and a construction exclusion zone drawn up with the relevant tree protection methods detailed on the Tree Protection Plan. Additional precautions outside the exclusion zone should also be taken around all retained trees.

For more detailed information on construction, ground works and specification see *Landscape Construction*, Volumes 1—4, by Fortlage and Phillips; *Landscape Architect's Pocket Book*, by Siobhan Vernon, Rachel Tennant, Nicola Garmory; *Landscape Detailing*, Volumes 1—4, by Michael Littlewood; *Specification Writing for Garden Design* by John Heather and others.

Ground Works and Construction Essentials - Summary

- *Tendering* — it is important that designs for sloping gardens are sent to contractors who are experienced in work of a similar scope. At least two quotes are advisable for comparison. Wherever possible, clients should visit similar completed projects before making a firm decision. Both designer and client must have full confidence in the contractor chosen to construct the garden.
- *Always check with local council planning departments* before undertaking significant excavations.
- *Drainage* — ground works and construction should take into account drainage issues. Creating surface water run-off into neighbouring gardens is unacceptable, either temporarily or permanently.
- *DPC* — in general soil must be kept 150mm below damp courses. Exceptions are when ramps are required for wheelchair access and a suitable barrier is installed. Timber deck-surfaces can be finished just below or at door-sill height.
- *Mature trees* should be protected during ground works and construction. Protective measures should be taken prior to the start of any work. Take advice from a qualified tree surgeon. Follow methods in British Standard BS5837: 2005 'Trees in relation to construction'.
- *Different soil types and conditions* affect excavation and construction methods; for example, sandy soil requires different foundations to damp clay soil. Check water-table levels before making design decisions, particularly if ponds or swimming pools are included in the design.
- *British Standards and best practice* — garden design specification should include details about best practice and safe construction methods, and BS references relating to materials including concrete and mortar.
- *Budget* — clients may require estimates of building costs in order to make design decisions. For this information refer to the latest edition of *Spon's External Works and Landscape Price Book*, edited by Davis Langdon.
- *Be on site* — nothing beats being present regularly throughout the project to monitor progress and answer questions. However accurate the plans may be, adjustments are invariably required when translating the drawing on to the ground during setting out, excavation and at key points during the construction process.

Paving and walls with luxurious planting around a circle create an outdoor 'room'.

6 STEPS, RETAINING WALLS AND ROCK GARDENS

Steps

Steps are integral to a sloping garden. They connect different levels but they are more than just a means of getting from A to B and circulating around the space. Garden steps are different from indoor ones: as a general rule their risers are lower and width wider. They have to be user-friendly to work, but this does not limit their design.

The shape, direction, materials and detailing of steps can alter the character or mood of a sloping garden. Steps add strong horizontal lines and dramatic quality to a garden design. They influence the tempo of moving around a garden: steep ones encourage a brisk transition; shallow steps with deep treads keep the pace slower; curving steps accentuate a sense of movement, suggest a meandering, leisurely approach and invite exploration.

All steps can be softened by abundant planting beside them; if this is required, allow space for plants to overhang without impeding progress up and down.

Lighting can be added to step risers for both safety and aesthetic reasons.

Handrails may be required on steep or long flights of steps, or where they are open on one side.

For more information on steps, see *Landscape Detailing*, Volume 2, *Surfaces*, by Michael LIttlewood.

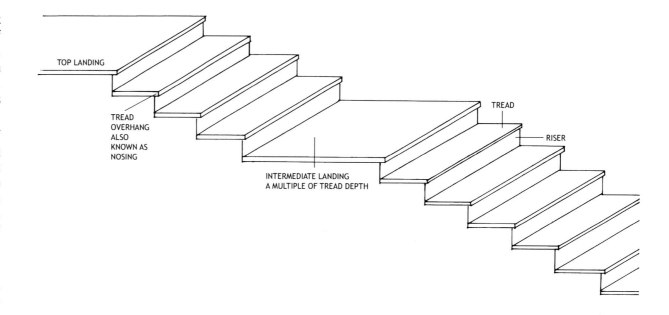

Figure 6.1 Step terminology:

Going — the horizontal distance spanned by the flight of steps.

Intermediate landing — a landing is provided on steeper slopes as a resting place, usually after 10 to 12 risers; the depth of a landing should be a multiple of tread depth.

Overhang — front edge of tread overlaps the vertical face of the riser; it is decorative, architectural detail that defines steps with shadow lines.

Pitch — the angle of the rise provided by the steps; safety and comfort dictate that this should not exceed 40°.

Riser — the vertical face of each step; each riser in a flight should be of equal height.

Tread — the horizontal surface of each step where the foot is placed.

A slight slope to the front of each tread ensures that water is shed.

Textured treads increase safety.

Guidelines for Step Dimensions

Aim for the ideal riser to tread ratio:
2 x riser height + tread depth = 66 cm (26 in).
Scale of garden, degree of slope and materials to be used make it difficult to adhere to a strict formula, but these guidelines are an aid to good step design.

Maximum number of steps in a flight	12
Preferred riser height	150 mm
Maximum riser height	200 mm
Minimum riser height	100 mm
Preferred tread depth	350 mm
Minimum tread depth	250–300 mm

Landing at top and bottom
  Same width as steps,
  and a minimum of 1200 mm long
Landing after 10–12 risers
  1–2 m, multiples of 3 treads'
  depth to maintain gait patterns

Pitch or fall: To avoid steps becoming slippery, a pitch or fall of no less than 25mm, either to the side or front will ensure water is shed from treads.

Figure 6.2 *Riser to Tread Ratio*

Minimum riser height = 100 mm
Maximum riser height = 200 mm
All risers should be of equal height
All treads should be of equal depth

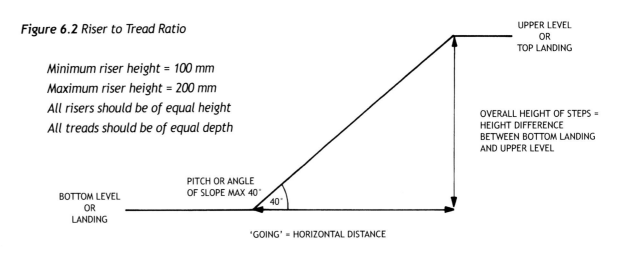

UPPER LEVEL
OR
TOP LANDING

OVERALL HEIGHT OF STEPS =
HEIGHT DIFFERENCE
BETWEEN BOTTOM LANDING
AND UPPER LEVEL

PITCH OR ANGLE
OF SLOPE MAX 40°

BOTTOM LEVEL
OR
LANDING

40°

'GOING' = HORIZONTAL DISTANCE

Figure 6.3 *Rule of Thumb for Acceptable Riser to Tread Ratios:*

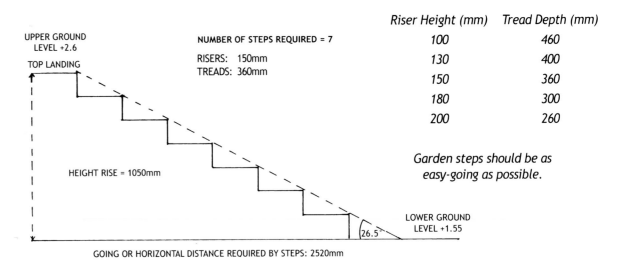

UPPER GROUND
LEVEL +2.6

TOP LANDING

NUMBER OF STEPS REQUIRED = 7

RISERS: 150mm
TREADS: 360mm

HEIGHT RISE = 1050mm

LOWER GROUND
LEVEL +1.55

26.5°

GOING OR HORIZONTAL DISTANCE REQUIRED BY STEPS: 2520mm

Riser Height (mm)	Tread Depth (mm)
100	460
130	400
150	360
180	300
200	260

Garden steps should be as easy-going as possible.

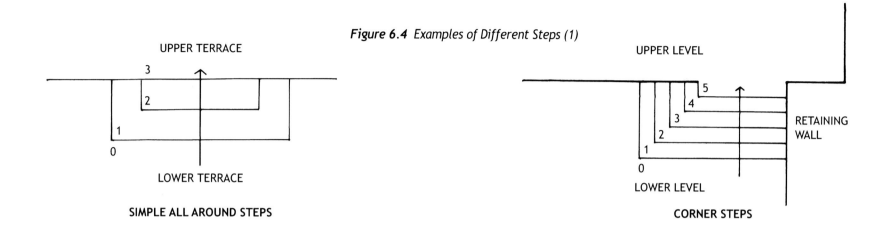

Figure 6.4 *Examples of Different Steps (1)*

UPPER TERRACE

LOWER TERRACE

SIMPLE ALL AROUND STEPS

UPPER LEVEL

RETAINING WALL

LOWER LEVEL

CORNER STEPS

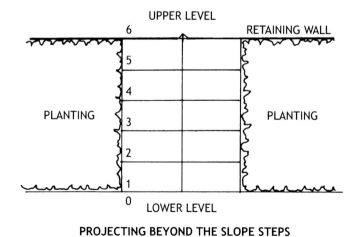

UPPER LEVEL

RETAINING WALL

PLANTING

PLANTING

LOWER LEVEL

PROJECTING BEYOND THE SLOPE STEPS

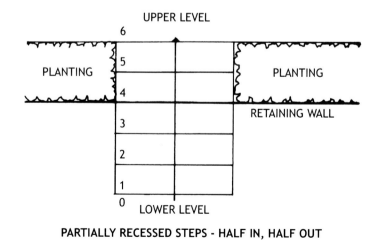

UPPER LEVEL

PLANTING

PLANTING

RETAINING WALL

LOWER LEVEL

PARTIALLY RECESSED STEPS - HALF IN, HALF OUT

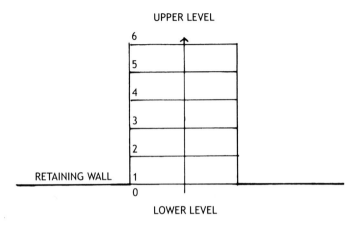

RECESSED STEPS - WITHIN THE SLOPE

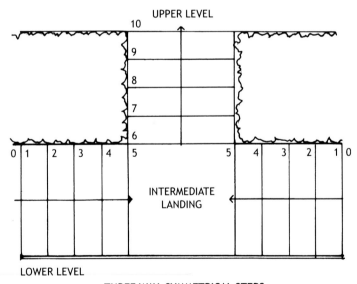

THREE WAY, SYMMETRICAL STEPS

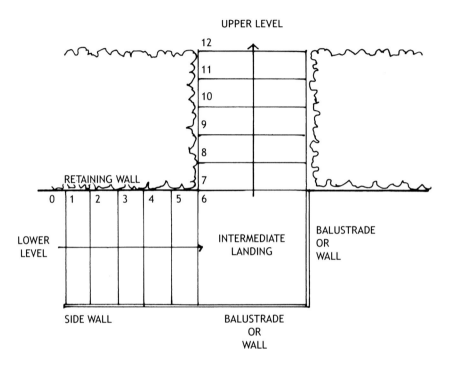

TWO WAY STEPS - FOR STEEPER SLOPES UPPER STEPS RECESSED, LOWER ONES PROJECT.
SPACE SAVING ON STEEPER SITES.

Figure 6.5 *Examples of Different Steps (2)*

Figure 6.6 *Examples of Different Steps (3)*

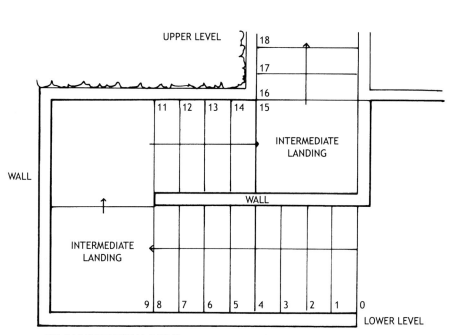

UPPER LEVEL

18
17
16
15 14 13 12 11

INTERMEDIATE
LANDING

WALL

WALL

INTERMEDIATE
LANDING

9 8 7 6 5 4 3 2 1 0

LOWER LEVEL

- ZIG-ZAG STEPS WITH LANDING
- ONE WAY TO ACCESS VERY STEEP SLOPES
- SPACE SAVING
- LANDINGS MAKE STEPS MORE COMFORTABLE

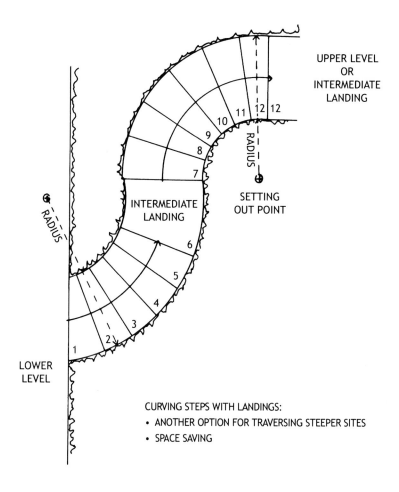

UPPER LEVEL
OR
INTERMEDIATE
LANDING

12 12
11
10
9
8
7

RADIUS

SETTING
OUT POINT

RADIUS

INTERMEDIATE
LANDING

6
5
4
3
2
1

LOWER
LEVEL

CURVING STEPS WITH LANDINGS:
- ANOTHER OPTION FOR TRAVERSING STEEPER SITES
- SPACE SAVING

Steps — A Summary

- *Riser to tread ratio —*
  2 x riser height + tread depth = 66 cm (26in).
  Important for successful steps as this ratio fits gait and foot size with both comfort and safety. The lower the riser the deeper the tread. Tripping occurs on shallow risers below 10 cm.
- *Long flights are overpowering* — add a landing every 10 to 12 steps if space permits. Landings are also required when steps change direction. This can be difficult to achieve in smaller gardens, but never compromise on safety or functionality.
- *Width affects mood* — narrow steps highlight the separate nature of the different levels that steps link. Wide expansive steps invite exploration of the garden. Steps with deep treads are a genuine link between two different spaces.
- *Shadows cast by steps* add drama and interest. Accentuate contrasts with overhanging treads, or keep treads flush for sleek, contemporary style.
- *Ramps* — continuous surface is required for wheelbarrows, wheelchairs and bikes. Ramps need 7 times more space than steps. For wheelchair access a gradient of 1:12, or 8% slope, is the guideline maximum, with 1:20, or 5%, a preferred figure. Minimum surface width: 1200 mm. Handrails: 1000 mm between. Landings at top and bottom of ramps: a minimum of 1200 mm is advised. Surface should be non-slip. These are guidelines and not always practical for smaller sites.
- *Ramped steps* need the space of larger gardens: risers 1 m to 1.8 m apart, with same gradient in between. Wheels can negotiate shallow ones. Useful where space restrictions rule out a true ramp. To keep it soft looking, use grass or gravel for ramp treads with timber or stone risers.
- *Safety* — handrails are required for safety on steep steps. Add handrails to steps as required by garden users. Lighting keeps steps safe 24 hours a day and adds drama to the garden at night. Lights at ground level are ideal and unobtrusive.
- *Planting softens* the line of steps. Wide steps can be used as staging for containers — decorated to enhance the whole garden.

(This page)
Examples of poorly designed steps which designers often face.

(Opposite)
Planting softens the sawn timber retaining wall. Decking leads to brick steps with timber edging.

Retaining Walls

Earth moved to create large level areas on a slope has to be retained. Avoid over-terracing a garden. Be mindful of the height of retaining walls, particularly close to the house, where views into the garden should be maintained as far as possible. Avoid creating boxed-in terraces and patios by positioning several lower retaining walls rather than a single taller one. Choose the type of structure and materials to mitigate their impact, and make them 'fit' both the design and the site. For example, in country gardens, use local stone; on more urban sites, match materials to those of the house. Seek expert advice for all retaining walls over 1m in height. Retaining walls have to hold back great volumes of soil and water, so need sound design and construction. Foundations must be suitable for ground conditions on site, the finished height of the wall, the materials used and type of construction.

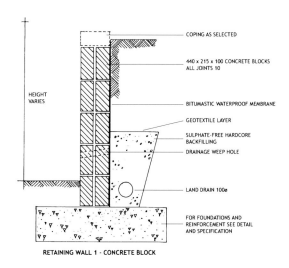

RETAINING WALL 1 - CONCRETE BLOCK

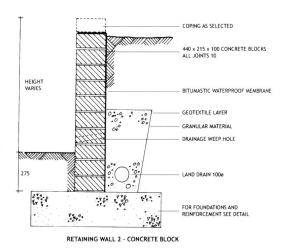

RETAINING WALL 2 - CONCRETE BLOCK

Figure 6.7 *Cross-sections of retaining walls using concrete blocks.*

Retaining Walls – Summary

- *Take professional advice* on retaining walls more than 1 m in height.
- *Drainage* – impermeable walls require drainage behind them. Install before soil is back-filled. Retaining walls made from materials other than dry stone or timber must have drainage channels through the wall to prevent saturation of the soil retained.
- *Retaining walls* are prone to frost and attack from sulphites caused by groundwater saturation. Choose materials suitable to site conditions and the height of walls without compromising the overall garden design.
- *More retaining walls may be less invasive* – building several lower retaining walls rather than one tall one on steeper slopes makes the garden more easily accessible. Step flights will be shorter and unlikely to create a boxed-in feeling.
- *Safety on terraces made by retaining walls* – a 900 mm-high barrier should enclose surfaces higher than 600 mm above surrounding areas. Options include railings, balustrades, fences, and toughened glass panels where the view is to be maintained. Parapet walls should be considered on slopes falling away from a level terraced area at the top of a slope. If this is near the house, choose materials that are in harmony with the building so that the structure is similar to a balcony surround rather than a too solid looking barrier.

For more information on retaining walls, see *Landscape Detailing*, Volume 1, *Enclosures* by Michael LIttlewood.

Rocks and Boulders

Some hillside gardens lend themselves to using large rocks to retain soil. A natural-looking stony hillside with outcrops of rocks that appear to be indigenous to the site is the effect required. Retaining walls can also be built to incorporate very large rocks; the more substantial in scale, the more results will give the impression of a real rock garden. This look is complemented by the use of natural stone paving for all other elements in a sloping garden: paved areas, paths and steps.

Using large stones, boulders and rocks when making a garden on a slope requires skill, but the results can appear a most 'natural' addition to the site and be at one with the wider landscape. This is particularly true where rocky outcrops naturally occur beyond garden boundaries, and where sites have only a thin layer of topsoil and rock is not far below the surface. When bringing rocks to the site, choose a type that resembles the natural bedrock in colour and texture. Match the shape of rocks and boulders to the surrounding types of landscape: use jagged rocks where the backdrop is of angular hillsides, and rounded boulders near the coast or at the bottom of valleys, where native rocks would have become water worn. Rocks and boulders that form an integral part of the garden design should be chosen with care: visit the quarry and select individual rocks with a contractor, who will advise on the size that can be brought to site and positioned by the machinery available.

A further complement to the use of rocks in sloping gardens is to make habitats for suitable alpine plants around and between rocks, and to create areas of scree garden at the base of retaining walls, rocky outcrops and cliff faces. For lists of suitable plants see Chapter 9.

Rocks used as steps at St Andrews Botanic Garden.

Gabions

Gabions are empty metal mesh boxes — like metal cages — that are packed with stones or other loose materials to make substantial building blocks that are used to form free-standing or retaining walls. On commercial sites, they are frequently used stacked in tiers that step back with the front of the slope that they are to stabilize and retain. In recent years their use in domestic gardens has become more common, and in some situations they can be a cost-effective way of building retaining walls in sloping gardens. They can be given a contemporary look by packing them with uniform sized and coursed stone pieces. For more informal results, fill them with random-sized rocks. Once filled, each lid is closed, secured with metal clips, and the gabion is attached to the adjacent units.

Retaining walls made from gabions are flexible so that they can adapt to an amount of ground settlement. Another positive attribute is their permeable qualities: water is allowed to drain through them, which can help deal with drainage problems on some sites. Plants can be included in the design of permeable gabion walls, and self-seeded vegetation will colonize these structures over time; this adds to their structural durability and also softens their appearance. By way of contrast this look may not be appropriate in a minimalist setting where permanent, strong clean lines match the design.

Gabions used for retaining walls at the RHS Garden, Hyde Hall.

Building Regulations and British Standards for Sloping Gardens

Building Regulations extend to the approach taken with landscape building work, and designers have an obligation to comply with the legal requirements. For full information for both sets of regulations, see:

www.planningportal.gov.uk/buildingregulations

Steps and Ramps: Building Regulations (Part M) relates to access to buildings including steps and ramps.
Handrails: Building Regulations (Part K) relates to protection from falling, and covers the requirements for handrails and balustrades, their position and dimensions.

The British Standards Institute (BSI) provides a comprehensive range of best practice solutions for all areas of services including the installation and construction of landscapes. Codes are defined in documents, each with the relevant BS delineation. The following two codes are particularly relevant when designing gardens on slopes.

BS 5395-1:2010 is the Code of Practice for the design of stairs with straight flights and winders.
BS 8300 covers the design of the approach to buildings to meet the needs of disabled people and includes details of lighting for ramps.

For fuller information see:
www.bsigroup.co.uk
www.standardsuk.com

7 GROUND SURFACES

The range of hard-landscaping materials available for garden making expands all the time.

Since 2008, the use of sustainable drainage systems (SUDS) has been subject to legislation that requires all new paving in front gardens to have a permeable surface. Given the heightened importance of drainage issues on sloping sites, it is advisable to follow these practices when designing new areas of paving in sloping gardens. This should ensure that excess water run-off does not create new problems on site or on neighbouring property.

For more information, see the Environment Agency website: www.environment-agency.gov.uk/suds

Design features such as rainwater gardens, gullies, storm-water planters and planted swales can combat drainage problems found in some sloping gardens.

For more information on water-management techniques in gardens and landscapes, see *Rain Gardens*, by Nigel Dunnett and Andy Clayden.

Ground Surfaces

- *Factors affecting choice of materials* in addition to the overall design: cost, function, ease of installation, ongoing maintenance and durability. Environmental considerations may also be a priority: restricting the use of materials such as concrete; reducing environmental impact by using materials from sources as close to site as possible or practicable.
- *Rainwater harvesting* may become more of a priority. Constructing a new garden is an ideal time to install these systems and may affect position of features, the materials used and the type of plants chosen for different areas.
- *Design harmony* — repeating materials used in the house is preferable, as is using indigenous materials such as local stone for walling and paving wherever possible, and where it matches the design intentions.
- *Appearance* — check how materials look in relation to other elements, in both wet and dry conditions. Weather can cause significant changes and also affects visual appearance of plants: check from the house and other parts of the garden.
- *Costs, budget and ongoing maintenance:*

Hard paving is the most expensive surface to install, but the least costly to maintain.

Gravel is cheaper but requires more maintenance to keep it looking good and usually needs replenishing over time.

Timber decking — hardwoods are more costly than treated timber softwoods; both require ongoing maintenance, as wood rots, splinters and is slippery when wet.

Man-made decking uses reclaimed materials. Some are wood free, and as the materials do not host algae, durability is longer and anti-slip properties are higher in wet conditions.

Lawn, whether turf or seeded, is inexpensive to install but requires high ongoing maintenance.

Artificial grass — increasing in popularity as a garden surface — is more expensive to install than real grass, but cheaper to maintain and possibly more durable; can be the only viable way to achieve a lawn on some sites.

Planting — soft landscaping is relatively inexpensive to install but has higher levels of ongoing maintenance in time and costs.

8 GARDEN PORTFOLIO

1. MOUNTAIN VIEW

2. QUARRY GARDEN

3. SUN CIRCLE TERRACE

4. THE RETREAT

5. PLANTSMAN'S GARDEN

6. LARGE COURTYARD GARDEN

1. MOUNTAIN VIEW

Clients were a professional couple who travelled extensively and wanted a low-maintenance garden. A shallow site always presents a challenge; invariably, the whole garden can be seen at once.

SITE INFORMATION

Size:	21 m wide x 9 m long/deep, 189 m²
Slope:	2 ways, up from house and from left to right boundary.
Gradient:	2 m difference top to low point behind house.
Soil conditions:	Average moisture, retentive, reasonable depth of topsoil.
Key existing features and plants to be retained:	Mature beech tree with TPO, beech hedge to back boundary; hedge top slopes up with the ground, garden shed to stay in existing position.

CLIENTS' BRIEF

- No lawn.
- Two separate sitting areas around the house.
- A water feature for sound effects.
- Leave space for a proposed conservatory to rear of house.
- A view point to appreciate vista of Cambrian Hills and surrounding landscape.
- Retaining walls — use local materials to reflect landscape.
- Working area required outside shed/workshop.
- Lighting.
- Planting — varied form and texture of plants combined with low maintenance.
- Budget — amount makes stone-faced concrete block walls feasible, with sufficient allowed for bespoke iron handrail and balustrade.

SOLUTION

Excavating almost the entire garden provided space for the conservatory and created a large, flat usable area around the house. Cutting and filling was not an option but the topsoil was saved for use in the borders. A sloping path leading to the upper terrace under the tree created an interesting circuit in a small garden and enabled the hedge to the rear of the garden to be easily maintained.

PLANTING

Shrubs and herbaceous plants with an emphasis on leaf texture and shape rather than colour were to be used.

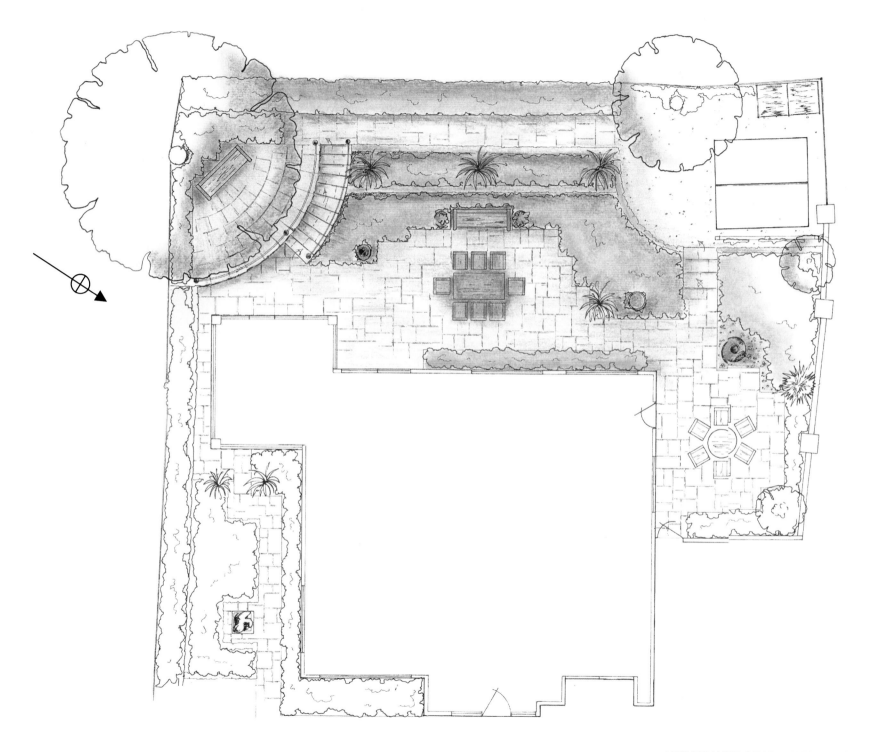

Before — Existing retaining walls and paving are uncompromisingly ugly and make a bleak garden view. There is no space for sitting outdoors in the garden in the current layout.

Before — sheds are often kept in their current positions as this one was. The slope appears to be encroaching on the house and the overall look is somewhat oppressive.

Before — a variety of different hard-landscaping materials do not give a cohesive look to the space. Uneven steps are poorly constructed with the top one a definite tripping hazard. There is no attractive space for sitting and enjoying the garden.

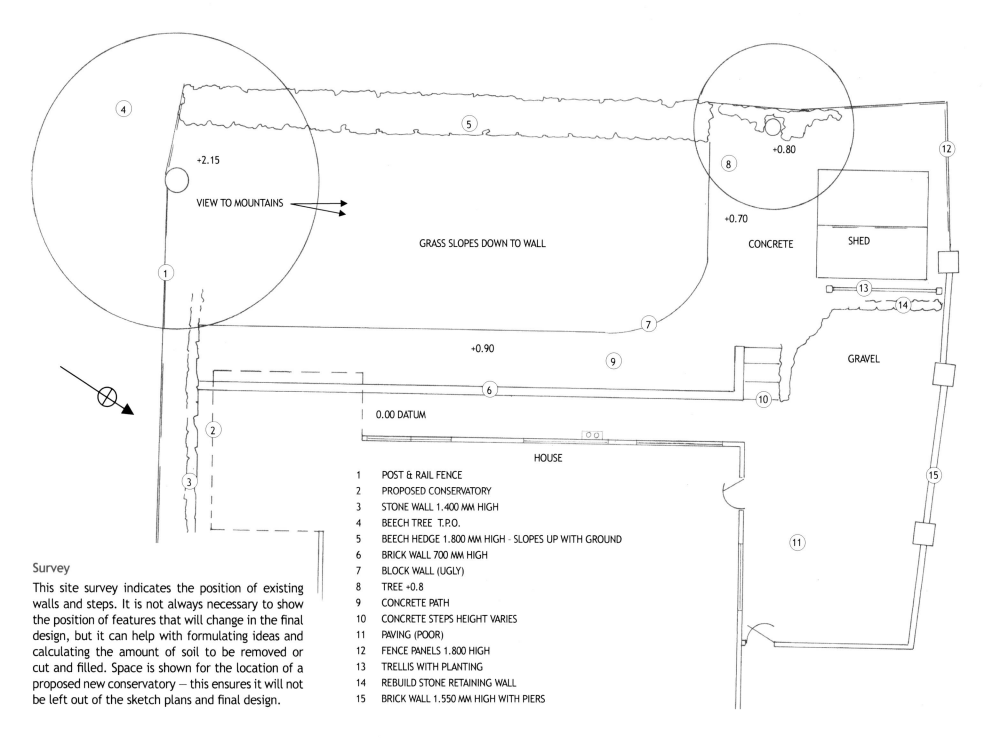

+2.15

VIEW TO MOUNTAINS

GRASS SLOPES DOWN TO WALL

+0.80

8

+0.70

CONCRETE

SHED

12

4

5

1

7

+0.90

9

13

14

GRAVEL

6

10

0.00 DATUM

2

3

HOUSE

15

11

Survey

This site survey indicates the position of existing walls and steps. It is not always necessary to show the position of features that will change in the final design, but it can help with formulating ideas and calculating the amount of soil to be removed or cut and filled. Space is shown for the location of a proposed new conservatory — this ensures it will not be left out of the sketch plans and final design.

1   POST & RAIL FENCE
2   PROPOSED CONSERVATORY
3   STONE WALL 1.400 MM HIGH
4   BEECH TREE T.P.O.
5   BEECH HEDGE 1.800 MM HIGH - SLOPES UP WITH GROUND
6   BRICK WALL 700 MM HIGH
7   BLOCK WALL (UGLY)
8   TREE +0.8
9   CONCRETE PATH
10   CONCRETE STEPS HEIGHT VARIES
11   PAVING (POOR)
12   FENCE PANELS 1.800 HIGH
13   TRELLIS WITH PLANTING
14   REBUILD STONE RETAINING WALL
15   BRICK WALL 1.550 MM HIGH WITH PIERS

Projection

Many designers today use CAD (right), and generating projections is simplified. Leaving out details, such as finishing materials and colours, helps designers and clients alike to fully understand the proposed changes in level. With complex sloping sites, they are an invaluable aid to accurate construction of the final design.

Hand-drawn projections (below) really help clients to visualize how the finished design will look. They bring a two-dimensional plan to life and do not have to be elaborate — simple overlays over a photograph are equally valuable and both types are very popular with clients.

CAD Projection of changes at Mountain View.

Hand-drawn projection of Mountain View.

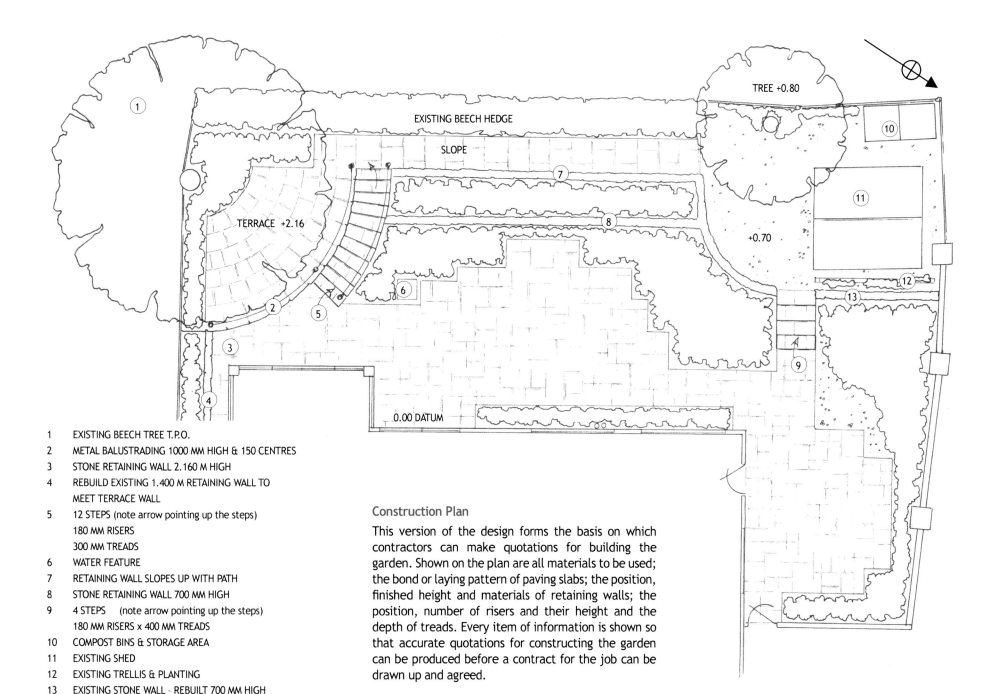

EXISTING BEECH HEDGE

SLOPE

TREE +0.80

TERRACE +2.16

+0.70

+0.70

0.00 DATUM

1 EXISTING BEECH TREE T.P.O.
2 METAL BALUSTRADING 1000 MM HIGH & 150 CENTRES
3 STONE RETAINING WALL 2.160 M HIGH
4 REBUILD EXISTING 1.400 M RETAINING WALL TO
   MEET TERRACE WALL
5 12 STEPS (note arrow pointing up the steps)
   180 MM RISERS
   300 MM TREADS
6 WATER FEATURE
7 RETAINING WALL SLOPES UP WITH PATH
8 STONE RETAINING WALL 700 MM HIGH
9 4 STEPS   (note arrow pointing up the steps)
   180 MM RISERS x 400 MM TREADS
10 COMPOST BINS & STORAGE AREA
11 EXISTING SHED
12 EXISTING TRELLIS & PLANTING
13 EXISTING STONE WALL - REBUILT 700 MM HIGH

Construction Plan

This version of the design forms the basis on which contractors can make quotations for building the garden. Shown on the plan are all materials to be used; the bond or laying pattern of paving slabs; the position, finished height and materials of retaining walls; the position, number of risers and their height and the depth of treads. Every item of information is shown so that accurate quotations for constructing the garden can be produced before a contract for the job can be drawn up and agreed.

During — Excavation has been completed and new concrete block walls have been built in their allocated positions. Local natural stone is used to face the concrete. Cabling for lights has been planned so that lighting on the steps will be both a safety feature and an aesthetic addition to the garden at night.

During — The shed is worked around during the construction process. Although isolated at this point, it will be integrated into the final design by the completion of the build and planting.

After — Only a growing season later: planting has matured and fills the border with lush, varied foliage forms and textures. Lush planting softens the expanse of paving and the visual impact of new walls. Covering bare soil with planting is one of the best ways to lower maintenance.

After — Sloping gardens offer scope for good aerial views down on to other parts of the space. Paving leads around the house, linking two distinct spaces.

2. QUARRY GARDEN

This project involved a new house constructed in a small quarry with its ground-floor windows looking straight on to the quarry face. With little light, the rear of the house was dark and depressing, and access to the top of the garden was difficult.

SITE INFORMATION

Size:	20 m wide x16 m long, 320 m^2
Slope:	Straight up from the back of the house.
Gradient:	2.9 m
Soil conditions:	No soil, poor drainage.
Key features to be retained:	None.

CLIENT BRIEF

- A garden that could be used!
- A contemporary design to reflect the clients' house.
- Sitting areas to rear of house and on the upper level to take advantage of the view to the mountains.
- Grass for young children.
- Safe water.
- Wendy house/shed.
- BBQ on top level.
- Lighting.

SOLUTION

The clients had already excavated the ground before calling in a designer. This is a fairly common occurrence. A minimalist block wall and steps that were rendered and painted echoed the design of the house. The walls and steps were painted off-white and pale paving was used to create a feeling of light. The retaining walls incorporated lit 'windows' that revealed either the quarry face beneath or a collection of 'curiosities'. A glass balustrade allows more light into the house and enables a view from both house and patio up to the top terrace.

PLANTING

Contemporary grass blocks, gravelled areas and mass-planted shrubs.

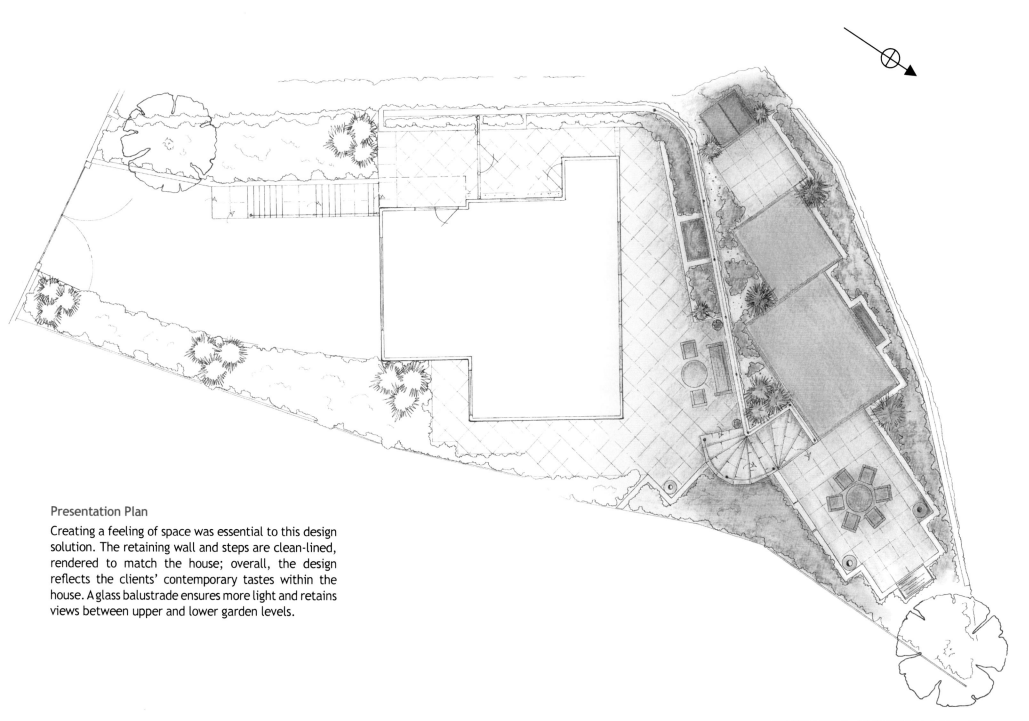

Presentation Plan

Creating a feeling of space was essential to this design solution. The retaining wall and steps are clean-lined, rendered to match the house; overall, the design reflects the clients' contemporary tastes within the house. A glass balustrade ensures more light and retains views between upper and lower garden levels.

Before — the sheer slope or quarry face was partially faced with stone.

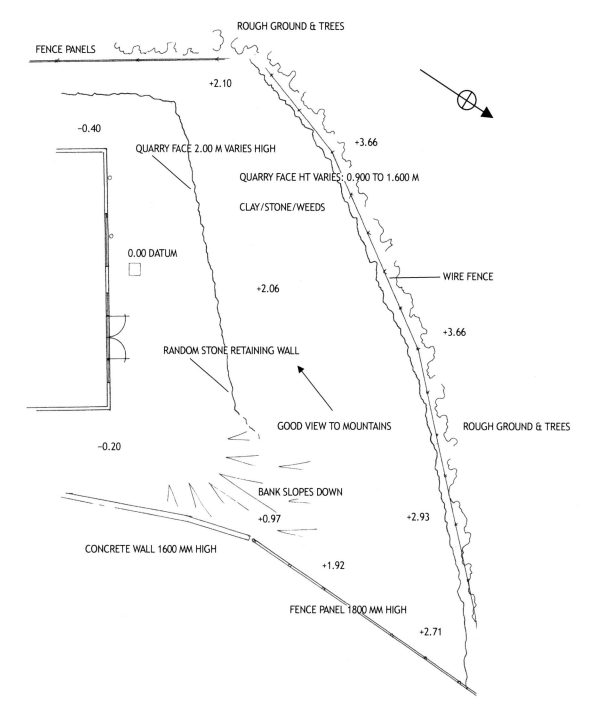

ROUGH GROUND & TREES

FENCE PANELS

+2.10

-0.40

QUARRY FACE 2.00 M VARIES HIGH

+3.66

QUARRY FACE HT VARIES: 0.900 TO 1.600 M

CLAY/STONE/WEEDS

0.00 DATUM

+2.06

WIRE FENCE

RANDOM STONE RETAINING WALL

+3.66

GOOD VIEW TO MOUNTAINS

ROUGH GROUND & TREES

-0.20

BANK SLOPES DOWN

+0.97

+2.93

CONCRETE WALL 1600 MM HIGH

+1.92

FENCE PANEL 1800 MM HIGH

+2.71

Survey

The quarry face overshadows the space, with parts of the top area 2.9m above the lower garden level allowing very little light into the ground floor of the house.

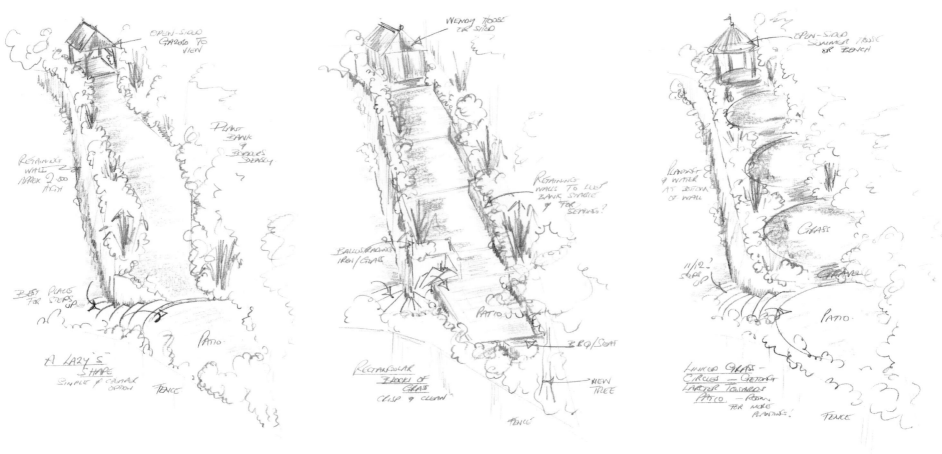

Rough on-site sketches for client.

Sketch 1

A very simple and cheap solution using a 'lazy S' curve with dense planting to soften the hard edges of the garden. An open summer house enables the client to maximize the view out of the garden.

Sketch 2

Rectangles fit well into the space, creating a more contemporary feel to the garden. Low retaining walls form sitting places and make maintenance easier. The shed/Wendy house is more practical in a small space.

Sketch 3

Graduated circles of grass linked by gravel paths create far more interest in the garden and allow for more planting.

1   PAVING FLUSH WITH BORDERS
2   POOL & WATERFALL
3   0.500 M HIGH RETAINING WALL
4   2.200 M HIGH RETAINING WALL WITH INSETS
5   360 MM HIGH RETAINING WALL
6   12 STEPS UP.
    180 MM RISERS x 400 MM TREADS (STEPS OVERHANG WALL)
7   BANK GRADED FROM TERRACE
    TOWARDS BOUNDARY
8   CONCRETE BASE FOR WENDY HOUSE
9   GLASS BALUSTRADING 1000 HIGH
10 SETTS AROUND GRASS CREATE MOWING STRIP & FORM EDGE
    TO GRAVEL
11 WALL STEPS — DOWN WITH GROUND
12 ANGULAR RETAINING WALLS CREATE RAISED BEDS FOR
    PLANTING
13 900 MM HIGH RETAINING WALL IN FRONT OF BANK
14 WOODEN SEAT BUILT INTO WALL
    WITH STORAGE UNDER
15 700 MM RETAINING WALL
16 BUILT-IN BARBECUE

Construction Plan

The working drawing shows all the information required
for a contractor to build the design, including proposed
changes in ground levels, the height of all walls, the
number and height of steps, materials to be used and
the finishes required.

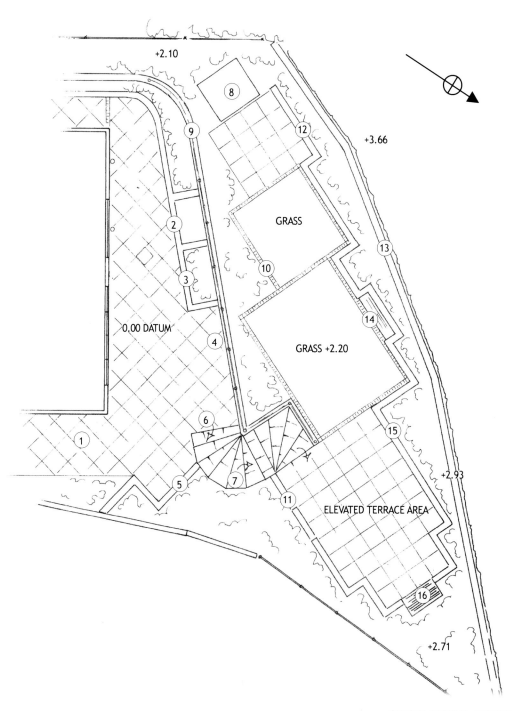

Elevation or Projection

White-painted walls and steps reflect light and enhance a feeling of space. Niches or 'windows' in the wall were designed to emphasize the quarry face by exposing sections and lighting them; others were destined to house interesting collections of found objects, fossils and sculptures.

After — retaining wall with windows of lighting above to illuminate curiosities, artwork.

After — built-in seat on the top terrace looks over the garden. This area receives maximum light. Angular borders make planting areas larger and bring colour and texture into the space.

3. SUN-CIRCLE TERRACE

This project was part of a much larger garden on a sloping site. Originally, the farmhouse was built into a steep slope. During a 1970s renovation a level area behind it was excavated from the hillside. Many years later the owners were able to purchase the neighbouring land that overlooked them along with a stone building that was used as a studio. This area was to be incorporated into the main garden.

SITE INFORMATION

Size:	20 m x 20 m approximately, 400 m²
Slope:	One way, up from house.
Gradient:	3.5 m above level ground behind house.
Soil conditions:	Neutral well-drained soil.
Key features to be retained:	Existing stone retaining wall to be extended.

CLIENT BRIEF

- Remove existing ugly block wall.
- Excavate ground and construct steps to upper level leading to a sitting area, allowing the sun into lower area next to the house.
- Upper terrace area to enjoy the view over the lower garden.
- Party area to fit 6m diameter circular tent.
- Maintain natural/wild style planting on the top terrace.
- Lighting.

SOLUTION

Extremely large quantities of sub-soil were excavated during construction. An imposing set of interesting, wide steps was constructed from stone and old flags to tie in with the existing wall and house. A new wall was constructed to a height level with the ground above, and an elegant iron balustrade was fitted thus allowing more light into the back of the house.

Creating a grotto large enough to walk into in the newly constructed wall under the steps added an element of surprise to the high wall. The grotto was constructed using tufa and shells from around the world. Pump-circulated water added further interest and helped the internal grotto walls to age. Large stones on site were used to create a rock garden above the wall on the graded ground.

PLANTING

Due to difficult and limited access to this part of the garden, topsoil was mixed with sub-soil during excavation. However, this was used to advantage by sowing a wild-flower meadow that would reflect the countryside beyond the boundary and using plants to encourage bees and butterflies.

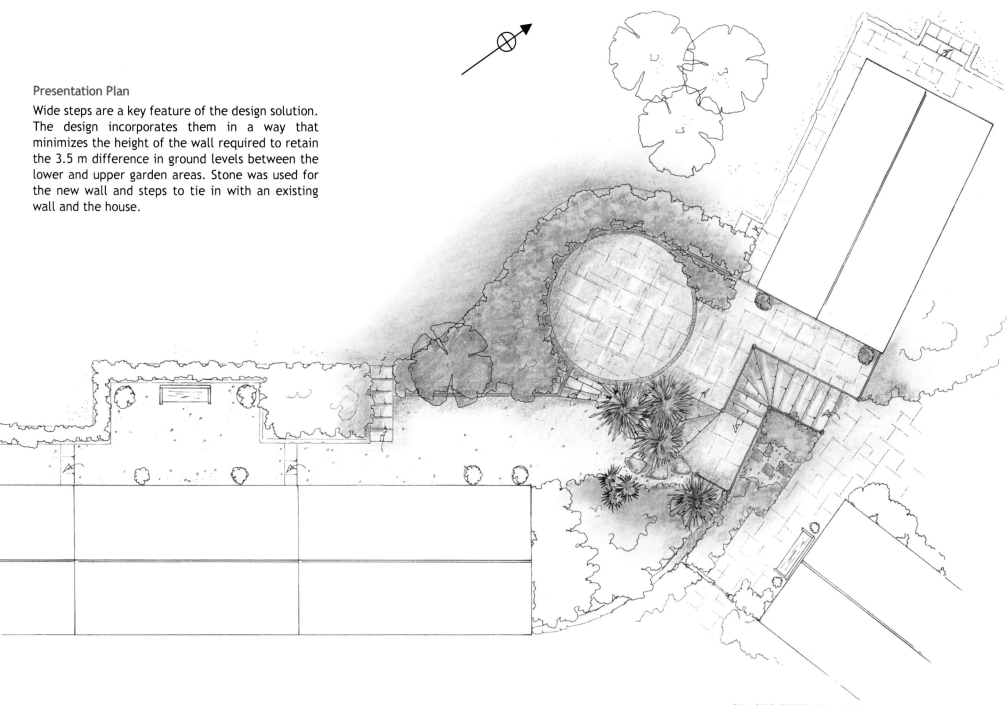

Presentation Plan

Wide steps are a key feature of the design solution. The design incorporates them in a way that minimizes the height of the wall required to retain the 3.5 m difference in ground levels between the lower and upper garden areas. Stone was used for the new wall and steps to tie in with an existing wall and the house.

Before *— ugly block and render wall is just 1m away from the house and dominates the seating area.*

Survey

A 3.5 m level change requires the removal of extremely large quantities of sub-soil. The priority here was to link the new parcel of ground at the upper level to the existing garden below.

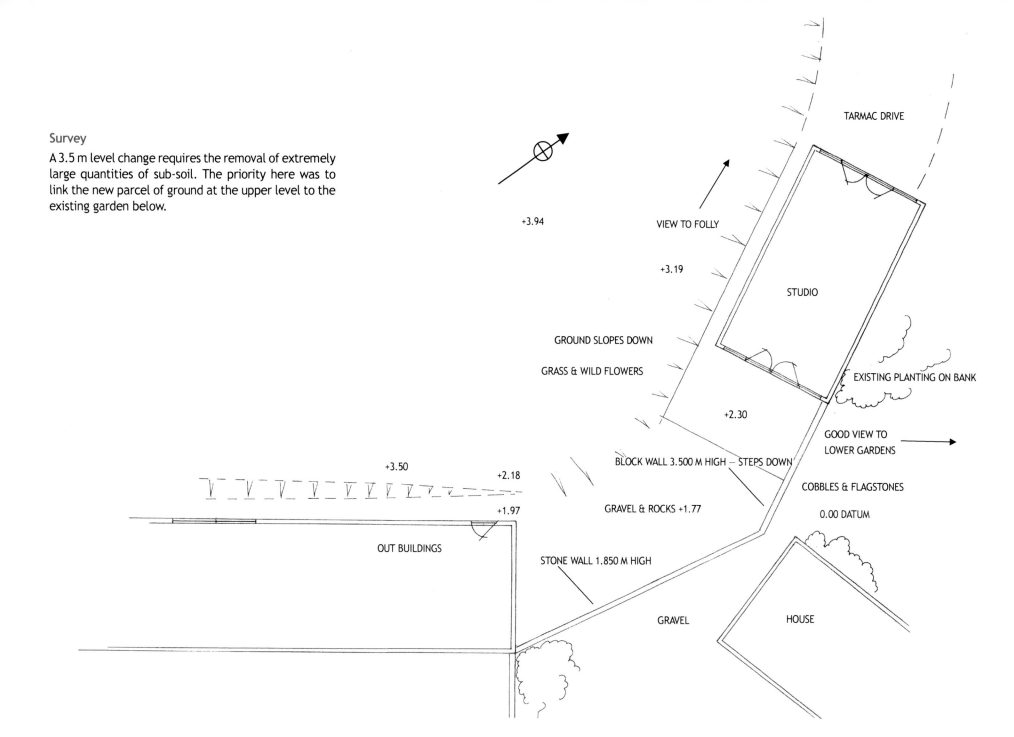

+3.94

TARMAC DRIVE

VIEW TO FOLLY

+3.19

STUDIO

GROUND SLOPES DOWN

GRASS & WILD FLOWERS

EXISTING PLANTING ON BANK

+2.30

GOOD VIEW TO
LOWER GARDENS

BLOCK WALL 3.500 M HIGH — STEPS DOWN

COBBLES & FLAGSTONES

+3.50

+2.18

0.00 DATUM

+1.97

GRAVEL & ROCKS +1.77

OUT BUILDINGS

STONE WALL 1.850 M HIGH

GRAVEL

HOUSE

Projection

Creating a large grotto adds an element of surprise in the tall new retaining wall and helps prevent it from dominating the space. Trickling water helps to age the tufa and shell construction as it circulates from the small pool below.

Constuction Plan

The number of steps, height of risers and their overall width are key items of information for contractors, not only for producing a quote to build a garden design but to act as an essential reference during the building process. Nevertheless, adjustments may still have to be made during the installation process.

1   6 STEPS UP:
    200 MM RISERS x 300 MM TREADS
2   CURVED STONE RETAINING WALL
    SLOPES UP WITH GROUND:
    650 MM BOTH CORNERS
    900 MM HIGHEST POINT
3   RETAINING WALL 1.00 M HIGH
4   3 STEPS UP:
    140 MM RISERS
5   ROCK GARDEN +1.80
6   3 STEPS UP:
    180 MM RISERS
7   GROTTO BUILT INTO WALL
8   STONE WALL & GATE
9   STONE RETAINING WALL 450 MM HIGH
10 STONE RETAINING WALL 2.300 HIGH
11 11 STEPS UP:
    160 MM RISERS x 430 MM TREADS

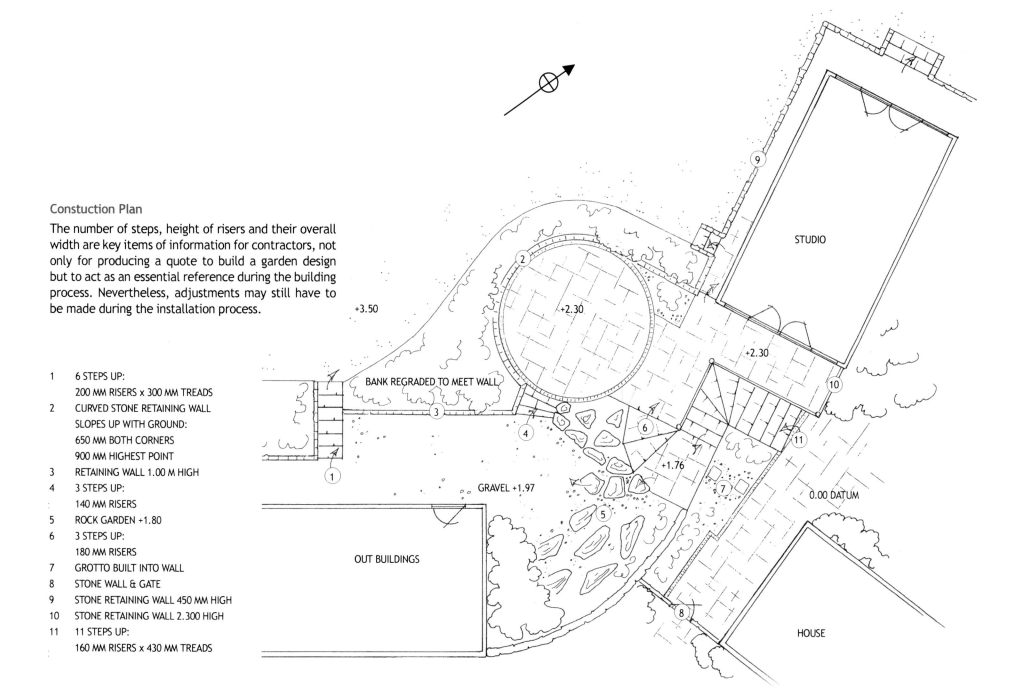

STUDIO

+3.50

+2.30

+2.30

BANK REGRADED TO MEET WALL

10

GRAVEL +1.97

+1.76

0.00 DATUM

OUT BUILDINGS

HOUSE

During — soil excavated from side of house to create a wider access allowing the stone wall to be extended, and the construction of steps and a small grotto.

After — late season colour and naturalistic planting melds with the meadow.

After — *newly constructed stone walls, steps and balustrading create an invitation to explore the upper garden.*

4. THE RETREAT GARDEN

The clients were a professional couple due to retire who wanted a garden in which they could work, relax and enjoy.

SITE INFORMATION

Size: 18 m wide x 15 m long, 270 m^2

Slope: A shallow slope from left to right and towards house.

Gradient: 2.4 m up from the house.

Soil: Acid, well drained.

Key features
to be retained: Well-established shrub border to rear fence. Five trees.

CLIENT BRIEF

*   Remove existing poor retaining wall and paving.
*   Summer house with sitting area in shade.
*   Sitting area near house.
*   Lawn.
*   Water feature.
*   Timber to be used for features.
*   Large borders.
*   Purple and yellow colour scheme for planting.

SOLUTION

Cutting and filling avoided the necessity of removing spoil and created four different levels setting up a journey through the garden. The existing brick wall was left in-situ and faced with new bricks. Placing the summer house under the existing trees at the end of the garden created a good focal point. Large wooden sleepers and gravel were used to create steps up to the lawn. Sawn lengths of timber formed an irregular retaining wall around two sides of the lawn.

PLANTING

A wide range of various shrubs, perennial plants and climbers with the colour palette restrained to purple/pink and yellow.

Presentation Plan

An existing retaining wall is rejuvenated with a different facing material to incorporate it into the new design. Two different styles of steps make the two-way slope more accessible: formal brick and stone slab ones lead to the focal point of the summerhouse; informal timber sleepers and gravel steps provide access to the lawn.

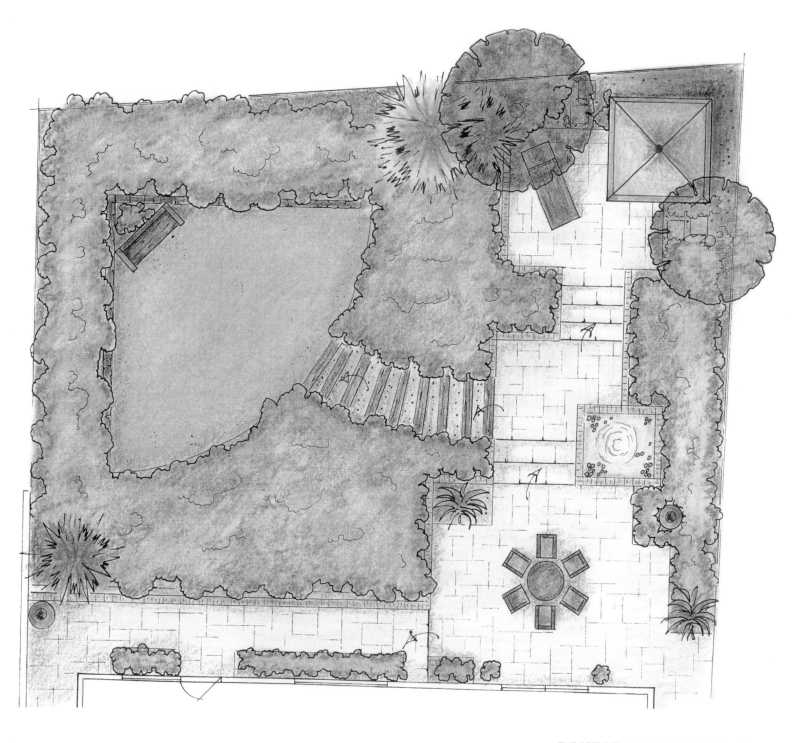

Before — low wall, sloping lawn and a scruffy, ugly fence.

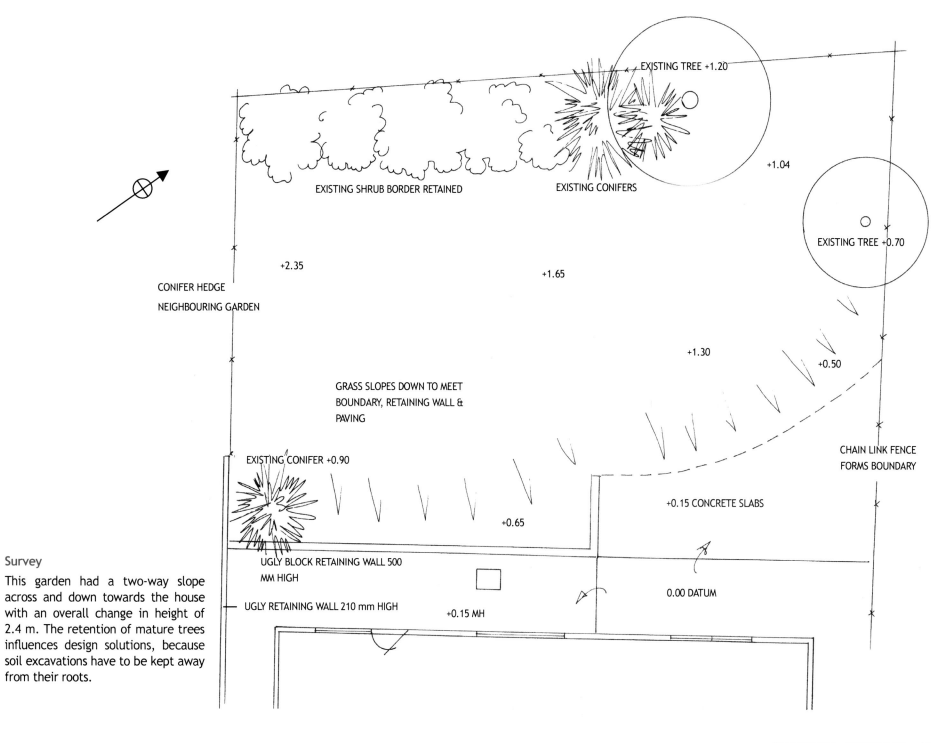

EXISTING TREE +1.20

EXISTING SHRUB BORDER RETAINED

EXISTING CONIFERS

+1.04

EXISTING TREE +0.70

+2.35

+1.65

CONIFER HEDGE
NEIGHBOURING GARDEN

+1.30

+0.50

GRASS SLOPES DOWN TO MEET
BOUNDARY, RETAINING WALL &
PAVING

CHAIN LINK FENCE
FORMS BOUNDARY

EXISTING CONIFER +0.90

+0.15 CONCRETE SLABS

+0.65

UGLY BLOCK RETAINING WALL 500
MM HIGH

0.00 DATUM

UGLY RETAINING WALL 210 mm HIGH

+0.15 MH

Survey

This garden had a two-way slope across and down towards the house with an overall change in height of 2.4 m. The retention of mature trees influences design solutions, because soil excavations have to be kept away from their roots.

During – brick wall retains soil and creates a raised pool.

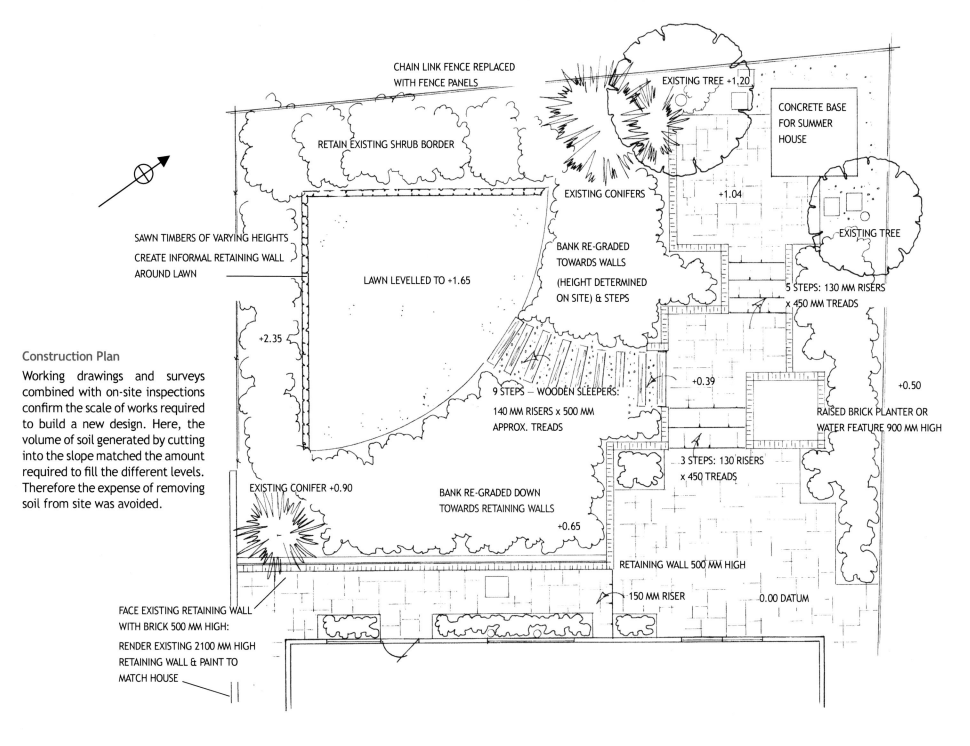

CHAIN LINK FENCE REPLACED
WITH FENCE PANELS

EXISTING TREE +1.20

CONCRETE BASE
FOR SUMMER
HOUSE

RETAIN EXISTING SHRUB BORDER

EXISTING CONIFERS

+1.04

EXISTING TREE

SAWN TIMBERS OF VARYING HEIGHTS
CREATE INFORMAL RETAINING WALL
AROUND LAWN

BANK RE-GRADED
TOWARDS WALLS
(HEIGHT DETERMINED
ON SITE) & STEPS

LAWN LEVELLED TO +1.65

5 STEPS: 130 MM RISERS
x 450 MM TREADS

Construction Plan

Working drawings and surveys
combined with on-site inspections
confirm the scale of works required
to build a new design. Here, the
volume of soil generated by cutting
into the slope matched the amount
required to fill the different levels.
Therefore the expense of removing
soil from site was avoided.

+2.35

9 STEPS – WOODEN SLEEPERS:
140 MM RISERS x 500 MM
APPROX. TREADS

+0.39

+0.50

RAISED BRICK PLANTER OR
WATER FEATURE 900 MM HIGH

EXISTING CONIFER +0.90

BANK RE-GRADED DOWN
TOWARDS RETAINING WALLS

+0.65

3 STEPS: 130 RISERS
x 450 TREADS

RETAINING WALL 500 MM HIGH

150 MM RISER

-0.00 DATUM

FACE EXISTING RETAINING WALL
WITH BRICK 500 MM HIGH:
RENDER EXISTING 2100 MM HIGH
RETAINING WALL & PAINT TO
MATCH HOUSE

Single planting of geranium softens the edge of timber steps.
Space in the width of new steps was allowed for planting to soften edges
and disguise graded soil.

After — *summer house overlooks garden and water feature.*

One season after completion, planting has flourished.

5. THE PLANTSMAN'S GARDEN

The client wanted a garden to indulge his passion for plants with space in which his grandchildren could play. This was a very steep site.

SITE INFORMATION

Size:	16 m wide x 30 m long, 480 m^2
Slope:	Steep, down from the left-hand corner on to a sloping lawn towards house.
Gradient:	5 m higher than area behind house.
Soil conditions:	Acid, with heavy clay.
Key features to be retained:	Four trees, greenhouse on patio, position of existing steps and compost bin.

CLIENT BRIEF

- Remove poor brick wall, high steps, paving and raised brick planters.
- Create a circuit around the garden to make it more interesting and for better flow.
- Potting shed near house.
- Large sitting area near house.
- Elevated sitting area to enjoy views.
- Large borders for planting.
- Level lawn for grandchildren.
- Remove lower hedge.
- Lighting.

SOLUTION

The existing brick walls were left in situ and faced with stone. The height of step risers was reduced and therefore the number of steps was increased to make the steps more comfortable and the garden more accessible. New larger borders reduce the size of the paved area making space for planting to soften the expanse of paving. The line of the retaining wall was re-shaped to accommodate more plants. Sloping lawn was levelled and the spoil was used behind the new stone retaining walls where the ground was re-graded to meet the top of the wall. No spoil was removed from the site keeping costs to a minimum. A maintenance path to the compost bin created a circuit around the garden.

PLANTING

Client's own choice.

Presentation Plan

Keeping existing walls saved on costs, but they were updated by facing them with stone to make them harmonise with the rest of the new design. Larger borders were cut into the existing paving to provide a better balance with the large expanse of hard landscaping.

Before — the paved area is a wide-open, bare space. Steps are too steep, slope of lawn restricts its use, and the garden lacks depth.

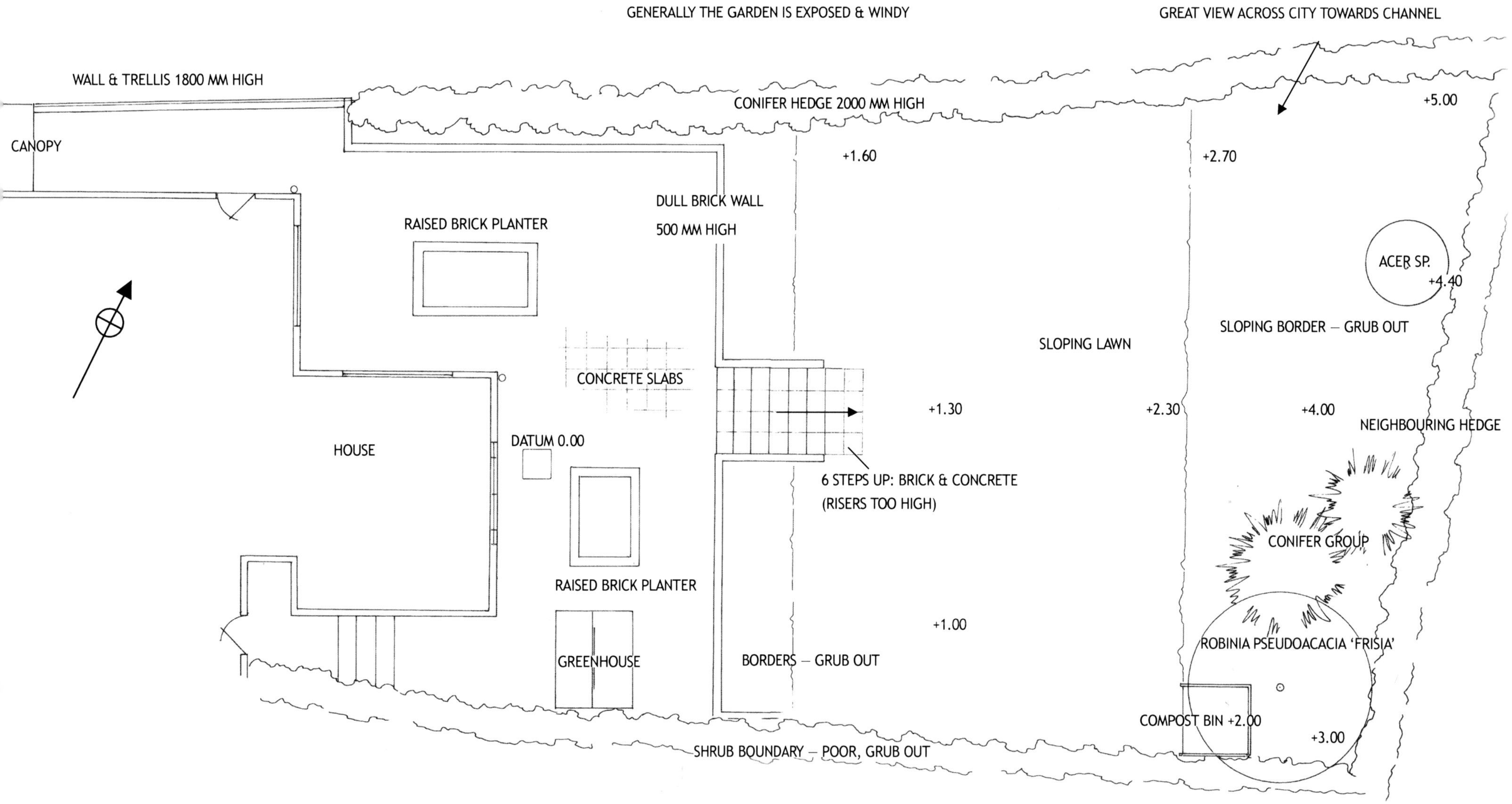

GENERALLY THE GARDEN IS EXPOSED & WINDY

GREAT VIEW ACROSS CITY TOWARDS CHANNEL

WALL & TRELLIS 1800 MM HIGH

CONIFER HEDGE 2000 MM HIGH

+5.00

CANOPY

+1.60

+2.70

DULL BRICK WALL

500 MM HIGH

RAISED BRICK PLANTER

ACER SP.

+4.40

SLOPING BORDER — GRUB OUT

SLOPING LAWN

CONCRETE SLABS

+1.30

+2.30

+4.00

NEIGHBOURING HEDGE

DATUM 0.00

HOUSE

6 STEPS UP: BRICK & CONCRETE

(RISERS TOO HIGH)

CONIFER GROUP

RAISED BRICK PLANTER

+1.00

ROBINIA PSEUDOACACIA 'FRISIA'

GREENHOUSE

BORDERS — GRUB OUT

COMPOST BIN +2.00

+3.00

SHRUB BOUNDARY — POOR, GRUB OUT

Survey

A 5 m change in levels is a very steep slope, particularly
in such a small space.

+5.00

VIEWING PLATFORM

EXISTING CONIFER HEDGE

SLOPING RETAINING WALL —
HEIGHT DETERMINED ON SITE

+1.60

600 MM RETAINING WALL

EXISTING WALL FACED WITH NEW
BRICK OR STONE 600 MM HIGH

BANK RE-GRADED TO MEET
NEW LAWN LEVEL

+2.60

EXISTING ACER

+4.00

1200 MM RETAINING WALL

+2.40

12-14 TIMBER STEPS UP
TO VIEWING PLATFORM:
200 MM RISERS

RETAINING WALL CURVES
AROUND & STEPS UP WITH BANK

8 STEPS:
150 MM RISERS
450 MM TREAD

150 MM RISERS x 450 MM TREADS
8 STEPS UP TO LAWN:
TOP STEP FLUSH WITH LAWN

+4.00

DATUM 0.00

LAWN — NEW LEVEL +1.20

RE-GRADE BANK TOWARDS WALL

EXISTING CONIFER GROUP

EXISTING ROBINIA PSEUDOACACIA 'FRISIA'

POTTING SHED

EXISTING GREENHOUSE

BORDERS GRADED TO MEET WALLS & LAWN

MAINTENANCE PATH — SLOPES UP

+1.20

+3.00

BRICK EDGING STEPS UP WITH SLOPE

Construction Plan

Existing steps were re-structured and increased in number to make them more comfortable to climb and to improve garden access. There was no need to remove spoil from the site when the lawn was levelled, and the results of this were used as backfill and to level the ground behind the new stone retaining wall.

REPLANT NEW BOUNDARY HEDGE

1200 MM HIGH RETAINING WALLS
FORM COMPOST BIN

After — (Above) A levelled lawn and bold groups of plants transform the middle terrace.

(Left) Steps lead up to small elevated sitting area.

6. LARGE COURTYARD GARDEN

Complete renovation of listed farm buildings including a large tithe barn and stables turned into one large dwelling. The courtyard is the only land on which the farm buildings stand, apart from a small parcel to the south and west. Principal windows and doors all face into the courtyard. A difficult sloping site where the buildings are on seven levels with many doors retained as features. The large barn dominates the site.

SITE INFORMATION

Size: 25 m wide x 35 m long, 875 m²
Slope: Ground runs down from the right to the left bottom corner.
Gradient: 3m from top to bottom, some cross fall.
Soil conditions: None — no soil, disused agricultural buildings.
Key features
to be retained: None.

CLIENT BRIEF

- Parking required on top terrace nearest gates to road.
- Working area outside workshop.
- Access to small gate at bottom of site.
- Terraced garden that will provide areas of interest and privacy.
- A number of sitting areas.
- Lawn.
- Possible swim-pond to centre of site to harvest rainwater from buildings.
- Pool for fish.

- Summer kitchen/BBQ area to catch last of the evening sun in bottom left corner.
- Use reclaimed stone roof tiles from the barn in design of walls or steps.
- Lighting.
- Year-round interest in planting.
- Easy maintenance.

SOLUTION

Level access at each door into the courtyard was a priority. To achieve this, seven different levels were created. Enormous amounts of subsoil and stone were excavated and removed from the site. With so many levels and steps the plan was computer-generated so that the client was able to easily visualize the garden from every angle. The smaller level areas work particularly well as they created more intimate spaces with a sense of enclosure. As a result, the whole garden cannot be viewed all together. Original old stone roof-tiles were used as risers in two sets of steps leading up to the tithe barn.

A centrally placed swim-pond was abandoned at an early stage in the design process due not only to high costs but also more importantly to an instinct that the site was already very grey. Building the pool on the bottom level proved impossible without having raised walls around it, due to the construction of a large land drain in that area.

PLANTING

- Mass blocks of tall grasses create rooms and corridors.
- Blocks of evergreen shrubs and all white flowers increase a sense of light.
- A beech hedge around the lawn on the middle terrace provides year-round interest in its different forms.

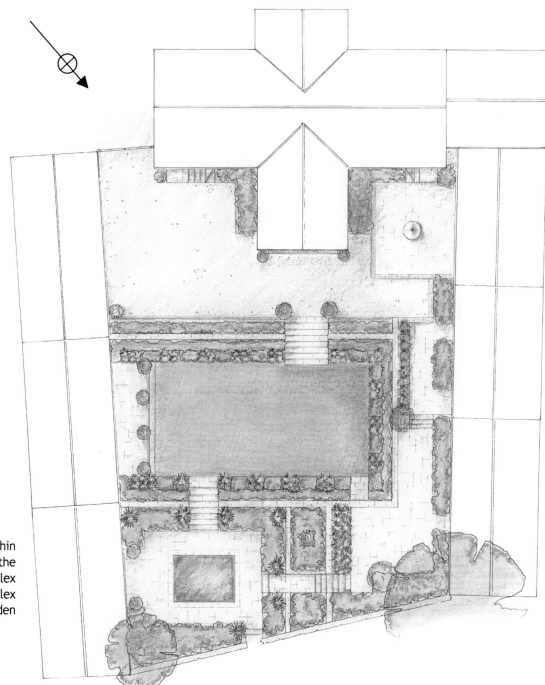

Presentation Plan

Seven different terraced levels within the site ensure access to each of the doors into the courtyard. A complex slope required an equally complex solution, although the finished garden appears to be visually 'simple'.

Before — a large derelict barn dominates the site.

Each building around the courtyard is on a different level, adding to the complexity of the site.

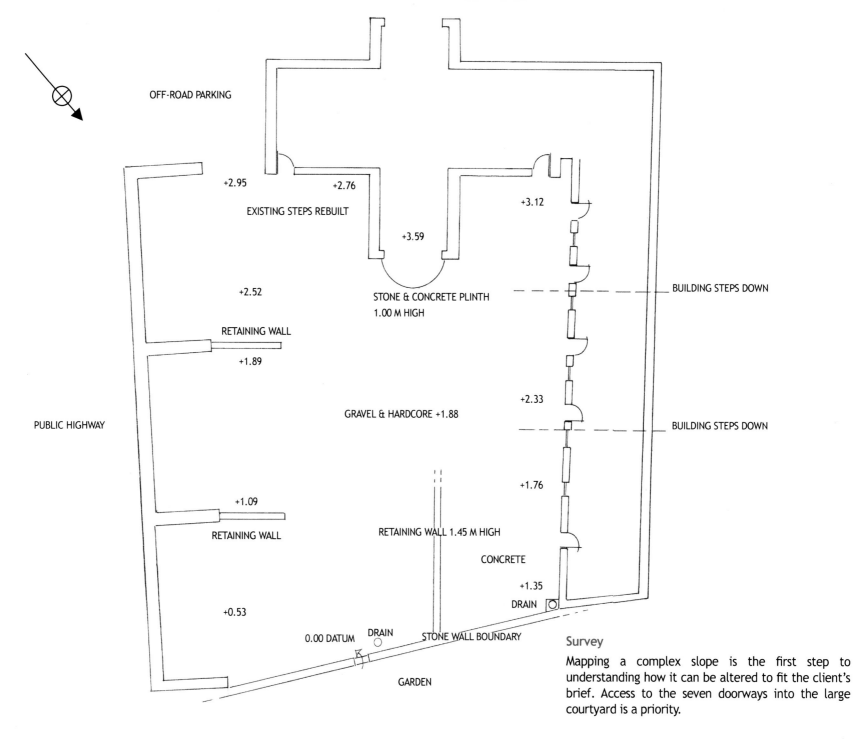

OFF-ROAD PARKING

+2.95   +2.76

EXISTING STEPS REBUILT

+3.12

+3.59

STONE & CONCRETE PLINTH
1.00 M HIGH

BUILDING STEPS DOWN

+2.52

RETAINING WALL

+1.89

PUBLIC HIGHWAY

GRAVEL & HARDCORE +1.88

+2.33

BUILDING STEPS DOWN

+1.09

RETAINING WALL 1.45 M HIGH

+1.76

RETAINING WALL

CONCRETE

+1.35

DRAIN

+0.53

0.00 DATUM   DRAIN   STONE WALL BOUNDARY

GARDEN

Survey

Mapping a complex slope is the first step to understanding how it can be altered to fit the client's brief. Access to the seven doorways into the large courtyard is a priority.

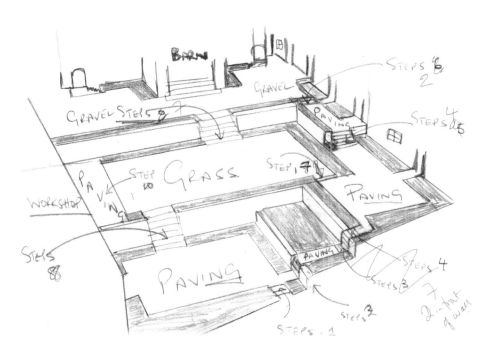

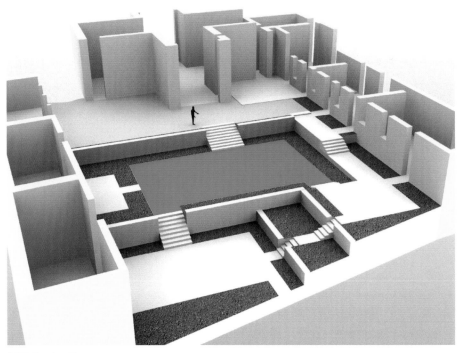

Hand-Drawn Projection

Hand-drawn projections are an enormous aid for everyone involved to gain a complete understanding of the site and proposed solutions. This one became part of the working drawings.

CAD Projection

A CAD projection helps the clients, contractors and designer to visualise the design solution from every angle.

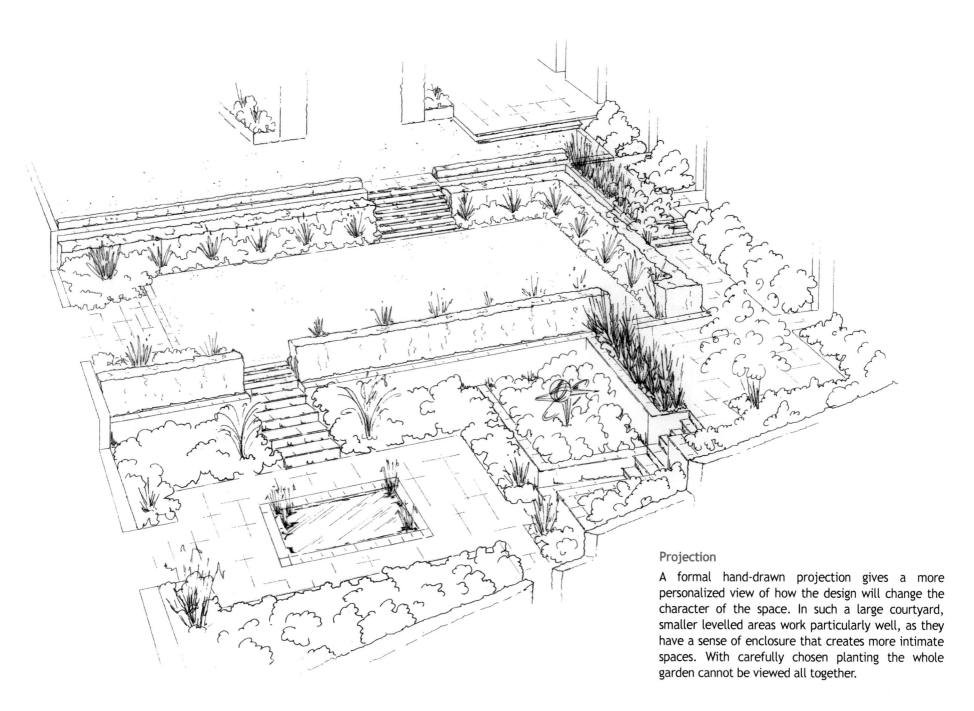

Projection

A formal hand-drawn projection gives a more personalized view of how the design will change the character of the space. In such a large courtyard, smaller levelled areas work particularly well, as they have a sense of enclosure that creates more intimate spaces. With carefully chosen planting the whole garden cannot be viewed all together.

During and After Construction — *the middle terrace walls are in place but steps to link levelled areas have yet to be built.*
Retaining walls are lime-rendered to match the original buildings. Beech hedge was planted in late winter.
View towards lowest point of the site (lower left).

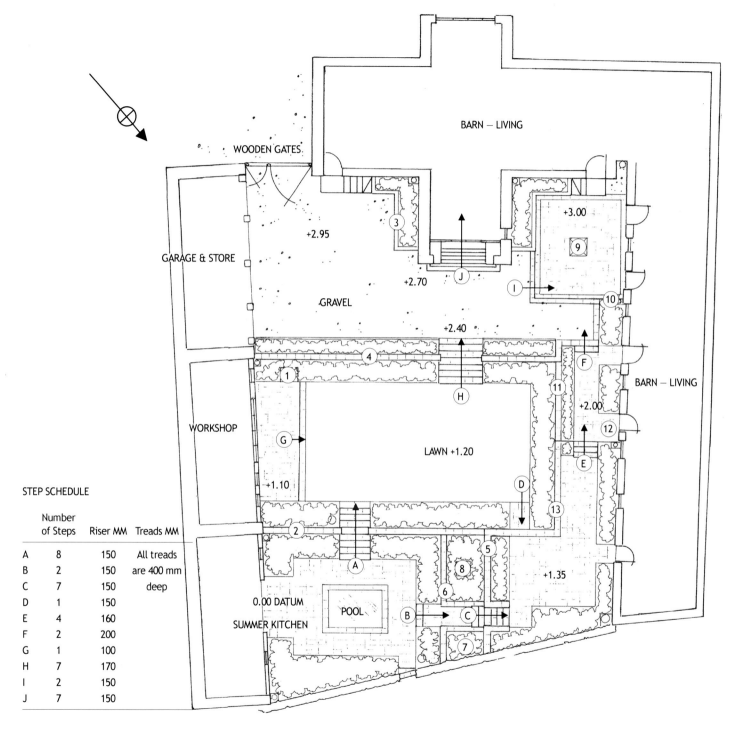

WOODEN GATES

GARAGE & STORE

BARN — LIVING

+2.95

+3.00

GRAVEL

+2.70

+2.40

BARN — LIVING

+2.00

WORKSHOP

LAWN +1.20

+1.10

+1.35

0.00 DATUM

SUMMER KITCHEN

POOL

1   CESSPIT
2   RETAINING WALL 1.100 M HIGH
3   RAISED BORDER 450 MM HIGH
4   RETAINING WALL 1.200 M HIGH
5   RETAINING WALL 850 MM HIGH
6   RETAINING WALL 550 MM HIGH
7   RETAINING WALL 400 MM HIGH
8   ART INSTALLATION
9   DOVECOTE OR TREE
10   RETAINING WALL 450 MM HIGH
11   RETAINING WALL 800 MM HIGH
12   RETAINING WALL 650 MM HIGH
13   RETAINING WALL 150 MM HIGH

Construction Plan

A working drawing helps to calculate which changes will match up with the total budget, and which may prove too expensive. Combined with the survey, it also indicates what changes are not feasible due to the presence of other necessary constructed features. Here, high costs, and aesthetics — the client and designer came to the conclusion that the site was grey enough already — ruled out the possibility of a swim pond; a large land drain constructed during renovation in the bottom level made it impossible to build a ground-level reflecting pool in that area.

STEP SCHEDULE

	Number of Steps	Riser MM	Treads MM
A	8	150	All treads
B	2	150	are 400 mm
C	7	150	deep
D	1	150	
E	4	160	
F	2	200	
G	1	100	
H	7	170	
I	2	150	
J	7	150	

After — *Various views of planting in the same season as construction.*

9 SOIL AND PLANTING ON SLOPES

Soil Erosion on Slopes

Soil erosion is a common problem in sloping gardens and may be compounded by the need to stabilise made up soil resulting from cut and fill. Non-woven geotextiles are one way to help control soil erosion on slopes. They are also an aid to solving problems of weed growth, moisture conservation and as a filter for sediments.

Examples of materials used in geotextiles

- Wire
- Plastic
- PVC coated mesh
- Polymer matting
- Jute matting – biodegradable
- Coir, coconut and straw – biodegradable

For soil stabilisation, geotextiles have three possible functions to perform:

1. *Separation* – prevents mixing of soil or granular layer with sub-grade.
2. *Filtration* – allows water to permeate from the subgrade.
3. *Confinement/containment* – restrains lateral movement of bottom of the granular layer.

For more detailed information on geosynthetics – including geotextiles and their use for soil stabilisation – see Terram's guidelines on ground stabilisation: **www.terram.com**.

Other erosion control products for gardens – refer to specialist companies such as **Hy-Tex**: **www.hy-tex.co.uk**

Planting on slopes

Plants provide a cost-effective method of erosion control on mild to moderate slopes. Choose plants with naturally spreading root structures to bind soil on slopes and banks. Lower-growing herbaceous plants and shrubs offer the best choices.

Plant density on slopes – more plants will be required to cover the ground. Multiplier guidelines:

1:1 slope (45°)	plan area x 1.41 (40% increase)
1:2 slope (26.56°)	plan area x 1.12 (12% increase)
1:3 slope (18.43°)	plan area x 1.05 (5% increase)

Alpines and other plants for rock and scree gardens

Acaena
Achillea 'King Edward'
Aethionema
Arabis
Arenaria
Aubrieta
Calluna
Cotoneaster congestus nanus
Cytisus kewensis
Dryas octopetala
Erica
Erodium
Helianthemum
Iberis
Juniperus horizontalis
Juniperus squamata 'Meyeri'
Phlox douglasii
Pinus mugo 'Mops'
Pinus mugo Pumilio Group
Saxifraga
Sedum
Sempervivum
Silene
Thymus

Plants useful for covering slopes and helping to stabilize soil

Ensure soil is weed free before planting. Planting through a landscape membrane restricts weed growth but can slow down the rate of spreading plant growth. On steeper slopes, covering the membrane with bark mulch presents the problem of keeping it in place. Battens are commonly used as a solution.

Acaena	*Phlomis*
Ajuga	*Phuopsis*
Alchemilla	*Pulmonaria*
Arabis	*Rubus tricolor*
Armeria maritima	*Sedum*
Bergenia	*Stachys*
Brunnera	*Symphytum*
Campanula carpatica	*Vinca*
Campanula portenschlagiana	
Campanula poscharskyana	
Ceratostigma plumbaginoides	
Cistus	
Cotoneaster dammeri	
Epimedium	
Fragaria	
Geranium	
Hypericum	
Lamium	
Omphalodes	
Pachysandra	
Persicaria affinis	

Grasses for planting on slopes

Choose grasses that have a rhizomatous growth habit - plants with underground root systems that naturally spread laterally - for speedier ground cover rather than clump-forming grasses. Plant slopes with a single type of lower growing grass for a natural 'lawn' on a slope that requires little or no cutting.

Carex 'Cappuccino'

Carex divulsa

Carex elata 'Aurea' - Bowles Golden Sedge

Carex 'Evergold'

Carex muskingumensis

Carex remota

Festuca - but plants can die out in their centres after a few years

Hakonechloa - beautiful movement in the wind

Leymus arenarius - sand dune native grass, good for sandy soils

Liriope muscari - purple flowers an added bonus in late summer

Luzula - good in shaded areas

Muhlenbergia rigens - needs sunny well drained soil, good taller clumps

Nassella tenuissima - great movement

Nassella trichotoma - beautiful airy flower heads

Pennisetum 'Little Bunny'

Sesleria 'Greenlee's Hybrid'

Sporobolus heterolepis - Prairie Dropseed, a clump former with good ground cover properties

FURTHER READING

Alexander, Rosemary, with Batstone, Karena (1996) *A Handbook for Garden Designers*. Ward Lock, London.

Brookes, John (1969) *Room Outside*. Thames and Hudson, London; reset and reprinted in 2009, Garden Art Press, Woodbridge.

Brookes, John (2006) *Small Gardens*. Dorling Kindersley, London.

Brookes, John (2002) *Garden Masterclass*. Dorling Kindersley, London.

Church, Thomas (1955) *Gardens Are for People, Reinhold,* New York; 3rd Edition (1995), with Hall, Grace and Laurie, Michael, University of California Press, Berkeley.

Davis Langdon, eds. (2011) *Spon's External Works and Landscape Price Book 2011*. Taylor & Francis, Abingdon.

Dunnett, Nigel and Clayden Andy (2007) *Rain Gardens*. Timber Press, Portland, Oregon and London.

Fortlage, Catherine and Phillips, Elizabeth (1992–2001) *Landscape Construction,* Volumes 1 – 4, Gower/Ashgate, Farnborough.

Greenlee, John, and Holt, Saxon (2009) *Meadows by Design*. Timber Press, Portland, Oregon.

Heather, John, *et al., eds* (2011, updated frequently) *Specification Writing for Garden Design*. Society of Garden Designers, Ross-on-Wye.

Humby, Ian, (in press) *Surveying for Garden Designers*. Packard, Chichester.

Irvine, William and Maclennon, Finlay (2005) *Surveying for Construction*. McGraw-Hill, New York.

Littlewood, Michael, *Landscape Detailing*. Volumes 1 – 4, Architectural Press/Taylor & Francis, Abingdon.

Lucas, Neil (2011) *Designing with Grasses*. Timber Press, Portland, Oregon, and London.

Reid, Grant W. (2002) *Landscape Graphics – Plan, Section and Presentation Drawing of Landscape Space*. Revised Edition. Watson-Guptill, New York.

Spain, Bryan (2008) *Spon's Estimating Costs Guide to Small Groundworks, Landscaping and Gardens*. Taylor & Francis, Abingdon.

Vernon, Siobhan, Tennant, Rachel and Garmory, Nicola (2009) *Landscape Architect's Pocket Book*. Architectural Press/Taylor & Francis, Abingdon.

Williams, Robin (1990) *The Garden Planner*. Frances Lincoln, London.

Williams, Robin (2007) *The Garden Designer*. Revised Edition. Frances Lincoln, London.

Wilson, Andrew, ed. (2004) *The Book of Garden Plans*. Mitchell Beazley, London.

Wilson, Andrew, ed. (2007) *The Book of Plans for Small Gardens*. Mitchell Beazley, London.

INDEX